DATE

DEMCO 38-296

THE SCHOOL ADMINISTRATOR'S GUIDE TO BLOGGING

A New Way to Connect with the Community

Mark J. Stock

Published in partnership with the
American Association of School Administrators

Rowman & Littlefield Education
Lanham • New York • Toronto • Plymouth, UK

Published in the United States of America
by Rowman & Littlefield Education
A division of Rowman & Littlefield Publishers, Inc.
A wholly owned subsidiary of The Rowman & Littlefield Publishing Group, Inc.
4501 Forbes Boulevard, Suite 200, Lanham, Maryland 20706
www.rowmaneducation.com

Estover Road
Plymouth PL6 7PY
United Kingdom

The original article from which this book is written has been published as
a chapter of the *Heart and Soul of Educational Leadership, Volume Six*, written by Mark J.
Stock. Published by Corwin Press, an imprint of SAGE
Publications in 2008. All rights reserved. Used by permission.

British Library Cataloguing in Publication Information Available

Library of Congress Cataloging-in-Publication Data

Stock, Mark J., 1957–
    The school administrator's guide to blogging : a new way to connect with the
community / Mark J. Stock.
        p. cm.
    Includes bibliographical references.
    ISBN-13: 978-1-57886-919-0 (cloth: alk. paper)
    ISBN-10: 1-57886-919-6 (cloth: alk. paper)
    ISBN-13: 978-1-57886-920-6 (pbk.: alk. paper)
    ISBN-10: 1-57886-920-X (pbk.: alk. paper)
    eISBN-13: 978-1-57886-921-3
    eISBN-10: 1-57886-921-8
    [etc.]
    1. School management and organization—Blogs. 2. School administrators—Blogs. 3.
Communication in education. I. Title.
    LB2806.17.S76 2009
    006.7—dc22
                                                                    2008028999

CONTENTS

ACKNOWLEDGMENTS

I heard the slight "tap, tap" of knuckles rapping on the doorframe to my office. I looked up to see Jim Evans, a trusted employee and a personal friend, standing in the doorway. It drew my attention away from the papers stacked on my desk. A quick glance at the clock on the wall revealed it was 5:30 PM.

I waved Jim into the office. Jim often did his best thinking at the end of the day when he started to unwind. Many of our philosophical discussions would start up as the office quieted down and the employees began trickling out.

I noticed he was holding a book in his hand. He reached over and tossed it into my overflowing inbox. I glanced at the cover, *Blog: Understanding the Information Reformation That's Changing Your World* by Hugh Hewitt.

Jim said, "Mark, I found a book you may be interested in reading. It may have implications for you as a superintendent." I could always count on Jim to challenge my thinking. He is one of the most widely read individuals I have ever known and his contrarian streak always made our discussions robust and interesting.

I took the book home that evening and thus began my journey into the blogosphere.

While reading the book I was struck by the magnitude of change that might be possible in this nation if public leaders reached out to constituents to communicate with them. I began to envision a community of readers and bloggers interacting through the social networking capabilities of the Internet, fueled by the captive audience that most educators have by virtue of their positions in the community. A blogger was born.

This book is centered on educational leadership mostly because of the personal examples I provide. Most of my blogging experience has come from three different blog sites that I have run over the years, all of them in the education arena. However, this book can be very useful for anyone interested in blogging whether they are in education or not.

Jim, this book is for you!

This book is also dedicated to my wife Sandy and my children Shannon and Taylor for supporting me in the various twists and turns that accompany us all on life's journeys.

1

BLOGGING EMERGES

SUPERINTENDENT AS BLOGGER

"Not me! Absolutely not me!" stammered Randy, my friend and colleague. The discussion at the superintendent's meeting had turned to blogging. "I get enough criticism as it is. I don't need another whacko taking pot shots at me from left field on the Internet," he added. He winced as he said it. "Why should I provide an easy forum for another critic?" he added.

"Randy, don't you think the rational folks in your school district recognize a whacko when they hear one?" I responded.

"Yeah, most of them probably do but I still don't want to lie awake at night wondering what the next critic is posting on the Internet," he responded.

"Do you lie awake now?" I asked with a smirk.

"Well sure! Doesn't every superintendent do that occasionally?" he asked. "I just don't want to make it easier for people like that to have a voice."

"I hear you," I acknowledged, "but what you don't realize is that now every person has a voice if they want to be heard. The explosion of Internet communication through blogging, websites, chat rooms, instant messaging, e-mails, and even text messaging means every Tom, Dick and Harry has a voice if they want one. The modern tech savvy superintendent recognizes that they better have a technological forum established *before* it all hits the fan and the whackos show up."

"Listen Randy," I continued, "If you have an Internet presence that's popular, educational, and already established, your rational public will bury your whackos when they show up. They get embarrassed by people like that who try to represent your community!"

"I don't know, Mark," he sighed. "I think my skin is too thin and my head is too thick to learn how to blog!"

I chuckled at his insight and added, "Maybe you better start blogging to them before they start blogging about you!"

He shrugged his shoulders and sighed. "You can't teach an old dog new tricks. I lasted this long, I can make it few more years."

I commented, "You might survive, but the new superintendent is expected to thrive, not just survive. Blogging is just one more potential tool in the tool box of the modern school superintendent."

"Well, then just consider me 'old school' then," he said with a grin.

I nodded and replied, "Old school I can understand, but while you're sipping margaritas in an RV park in Arizona, our younger colleagues are going to be on the front lines. Who knows what challenges they will face? If we don't find new ways of getting the good word out about public education, the term 'old school' might mean more than you think!"

As the meeting ended and we went our separate ways, I wondered once again what the future would hold for superintendents on the front lines of the war on public education.

WHAT'S A BLOG?

The word "blog" is relatively new and like most new technology terms, you might not find it in your spell checker or your dictionary yet. The word blog comes from combining the words "web" (short for World Wide Web) and the word "log" (indicating a regular entry). A blog therefore, is a website that is updated regularly with a variety of content. Blogging is the act of journaling on a regular basis on the Internet. A blogger is the person posting the main information found on the site.

The number and the type of blogs available on the Internet are limited only by the imagination of the bloggers. There are political blogs, technology blogs, family blogs, sports blogs, quilting blogs, housewife blogs, school blogs, teacher blogs, and even satire blogs. If you have thought about it, then someone is blogging about it. These blogs can be open to everyone to read, or open to only those you invite. These blogs can be open to commentary or closed to reader comments. They can be open to comment only on selected postings or open to every posting. You can even set up your blog to approve comments before they get posted. There are many options available to the blogger depending on the purpose and scope of the blog. However, the one major characteristic that all good blogs have in common is that they post a variety of content to the Internet on a frequent or regular basis.

COMMON CHARACTERISTICS OF BLOGS

Most blogs have a number of common characteristics. These include a main content area with articles listed chronologically with the most recent posts on top. The articles are often organized into categories so that blog readers can search the archives based on the topics of interest. Most blogs also carry an archive of older articles. These can be searched by topic and allow the blog reader to locate information of interest that has been organized by topic.

Another common characteristic of most blogs is that they often provide a way for people to leave comments about the articles that are posted. This interaction is often one of the attractive features that make blogs different from websites.

Blogs also provide a list of links to other related sites, sometimes called a *blogroll*. These links allow blog readers to navigate from one site to another based on common interests.

Another characteristic common to blog sites is that they often provide one or more "feeds" like RSS, Atom, or RDF files. These feeds allow the active blog reader to be notified when their blogs of interest have been updated. Many blog experts believe that the future of blogging lies in some modification of this feature. This allows the active blog reader to be notified when their blogs have been changed, freeing them from having to remember to check the sites frequently. This level of personalization and customization appears to be a future trend. So how is blogging as a school leader different from just keeping your website current?

One of the most important benefits to blogging for the school administrator comes from interacting with the community. While most websites are fairly static and in many cases even out of date, blog sites are frequently updated. A successful blog site is updated frequently if not daily, so that when a patron logs on they expect to see something new. This actually reinforces frequent visits to the site. A patron who accesses a site two or three times and does not find new information is less likely to return to the site. Because most successful bloggers allow visitors to leave comments, it is highly likely that a frequent visitor will find something new, even if it is only found in the comment sections of the blog. This is the theory of intermittent reinforcement. When the patron finds something new then they are rewarded for their efforts and they are more likely to return again.

This interaction between the blogger and visitors leaving comments is one of the features that distinguish blogging from other websites. When a blog site moderator allows visitors to interact by discussing their opinions and reactions to the postings, it creates a vibrant online community that not only attracts more visitors but also encourages more frequent visits to the site. Those "whackos" my friend Randy was worrying about are actually one of the magnetic forces that pulls visitors to the site. Just because you never heard that strange voice doesn't mean that it hasn't always existed. Many rational people are actually shocked to find out that there are people with such unusual viewpoints.

The daily posting of new content and the interaction of online readers are two of the main features that distinguish a blog site from traditional school websites. This interaction with the public can offer tremendous benefits not only for the community but for the superintendent or educational leader as well.

Another way that blog sites are different than websites is the style and language they are written in. Blogs are usually written in a personal voice allowing glimpses into the personality of the author. Websites are more likely to contain formal documents, forms, and content specific to the website's purpose. Because blogs normally involve daily interaction with others they tend to have a more personal flavor.

Blog sites are also more widely distributed than websites. This is usually because the amount of traffic on a blog can be potentially high due to the daily and weekly updates and the interaction between the host and those leaving comments.

I received the following e-mail from a local parent that touches on a few of these benefits that blogs can provide. As you read this e-mail and other examples provided in this book, note the personal touch that the blogging forum appears to foster. While there are some disadvantages to blogging, the interaction with the public almost always provides an overall positive impact on the community.

> *Mrs. R.'s e-mail to Dr. Stock:*
> *Hi there! I just wanted to tell you how much I appreciate your site. I have been having fun with the comments about special education. I guess I'm pretty see-through to anyone who really knows me. Mrs. H. and Miss H. already figured me out as the anon who is so opinionated and always defending the school. I hope I haven't posted anything out of line and if so, please let me know. People just drive me crazy at how ignorant they are at how funding and such works.*
>
> *I really enjoy reading your posts about all topics. They are very informative. Thanks for taking the time to do this. It's nice to feel like I know you, even if we have never met. You make me feel like you view yourself more as an equal to the community and not just all about power. LOL!! That sounded funny, hope you don't take that the wrong way.*
>
> *BTW, if you have ever been to the school, I'm sure you know my son, Z. He's the really loud kid in Miss H's class. He is quite the character and has a way of bringing a smile to the faces of the most bitter people.*
> *Thanks again,*
> *Mrs. R.*

Throughout the remainder of this book we will continue to lay out the benefits, drawbacks and methodologies to blogging as a school leader and share more examples of blogging in action.

Let's start by taking a brief look at the history of blogging. Where did it come from and how did blogging emerge as a technological innovation?

HISTORY OF BLOGGING

Blogs are not as new as people think, but their popularity is a recent phenomenon. In 1999 there weren't very many blogs but today there are millions of them. How did this come about?

In an attempt to make their own blogging efforts easier, early bloggers created user-friendly tools that made blogging simple. In the infant stages of blogging you needed to know a lot about the Internet, computers, and the technical computer language used for creating websites in order to create and maintain a blog. Today, you can get started with little more than an e-mail address, a computer, and an Internet connection. Searching the Internet for free blogging software will get you started very quickly. Blogger.com launched in 1999 and is now widely regarded as the largest and most popular of the free blog sites.

The advent of such free and user-friendly software has made blogging an easy task even for the newbie. While blogging well is somewhat complex, creating a simple blog site is now as easy as making a few menu selections from your choice of blogging software.

So how did all this begin? Although there are some occasional skirmishes among techies over who was first and who was second, there is general agreement among most bloggers over the key points in blogging history.

HISTORICAL TIMELINE OF BLOGGING

1. Dawn of the Internet: Tim Berners-Lee, father of the World Wide Web, begins keeping a list of new sites as they come on line. This could be the early form of the current blogger practice of providing links to other sites from their blog site.

2. January, 1994: Justin Hall launches Justin's Home Page which would become Links from the Underground
3. April, 1997: Dave Winer launches Scripting News.
4. December, 1997: Jorn Barger coins the term *web log*.
5. Early 1999: Peter Merholz coins the term *blog* after announcing he was going to pronounce web logs as "Weeblog." This was shortened to blog.
6. July, 1999: Pitas launches the first free build-your-own blog web tool.
7. August, 1999: Blogger is released and becomes the most popular web-based blogging tool. Blogging is popularized with mainstream Internet users.
8. February, 2002: Heather Armstrong is fired for discussing her job on her blog "Dooce." "Dooced" becomes a verb meaning "fired for blogging."
9. August, 2002: Blogads launches as the first broker of blog advertising.
10. December, 2002: The blog "Talking Points Memo" highlights Trent Lott's racially charged comments and two weeks later Lott resigns from his post as Senate majority leader. Blogging is now a political influence.
11. June, 2003: Google launches AdSense, which matches ads to blog content.
12. August, 2003: The first barrage of ads on political blogs occurs.
13. December, 2004: Merriam-Webster declares *blog* the "Word of the Year."
14. January, 2005: A study shows that 32 million Americans read blogs.
15. December, 2005: An estimated $100 million worth of blog ads are sold.

The blogging phenomenon has grown with the same explosiveness as many other technological innovations. And like most trends, blogs are new enough to be hip, but what is it about blogging that brings people back again and again?

WHY DO PEOPLE BLOG?

There are many reasons people blog, but one of the biggest is to provide a wider forum for their thoughts and to connect with other people interested in the same subjects. E. M. Forster is widely credited with the quotation, "How do I know what I think until I see what I say?" This sums up the common experience of many active bloggers. The very act of writing seems to crystallize the many thoughts that often bounce around inside our heads in a random and often unexamined way. Blogging for many people goes well beyond a communication tool for work or family, it often becomes a personally enlightening activity that helps them formulate and summarize the many thoughts and ideas that rumble around upstairs. On many occasions as an active blogging superintendent, I would find myself puzzling over a post before hitting the "publish" button, thinking, "Do I really believe this? Is this the essentially important concept? What is my personal philosophy on this?"

One of the most recent uses for blogging is a direct result of how mobile our society has become. Because so many families today live and travel in different parts of the world for various lengths of time, blogging has emerged as a method of keeping in touch with family and friends. Instead of the annual Christmas card summary of all that has happened in a year, many families are posting pictures and stories as they experience them so they can keep everyone up-to-date. This could be everything from an expedition to the North Pole, to grandma's first visit to Europe. Blogging has provided an easy way for friends and family to stay in touch no matter where they are.

CHAPTER 1

The advent of the so called "mommy blogs" has been another recent phenomenon that shows the power of the Internet's social networking abilities. Mommy blogs are blogs that mothers have created in order to share information, stories, and knowledge. They allow the stay-at-home mom to feel less isolated and more connected to other mothers. When you think about the mobile society we have today and the fact that there are very few extended families that live in close proximity to each other, it is easy to see how the social networking of the Internet would provide a sense of emotional connection for many mothers.

Another interesting aspect of the "mommy blog" is the economic power that these socially networked moms possess. They are trusted for their practical opinions on products, services, and ideas and are often the primary buyers for all goods and services in the home. The economic power of these networked mothers, who blog about the products and services they use, is a force that marketing professionals cannot ignore. As the Internet traffic on these blogs has increased, the advertising agencies have taken notice.

And don't forget the importance of grandma! Mothers that are not in close proximity to their parents can still keep grandma and grandpa in the loop on little Johnny's first words by filming them and posting a video clip on the blog so grandma can enjoy it too. The popularity of mommy blogs is another example of the networking potential of the Internet filling an emotional need in our society as the extended family spreads out across the world.

Like many trends, blogging has been picked up quite readily by the younger generations. While the young have always wanted to leave their mark on the world, the development of blogging software has created an easy-to-use forum that allows the blogger to have a worldwide soap box to stand on. Do you remember as a youth when you sought to leave your mark on the world by using your red Swiss army knife to carve your initials into the tree in your backyard? Do you remember when you dragged your stick through the wet cement in the new sidewalk, leaving a message for all who passed by? Well, our children and grandchildren are seeking to leave their mark on the world electronically. They use social networking and blogging software to post their thoughts and views for the world to see. And just like the initials in the tree or the words on the sidewalk that seemed to last forever, so often the digital footprints left by today's generation seem to last forever.

In addition to young people and mothers blogging, another group that has stormed the blogosphere are those interested in politics. Not only are political blogs popular, but they may have forever changed the political landscape. Many pundits believe that John Kerry's presidential bid in 2004 was torpedoed by critics of his Vietnam War record. Much of the criticism sped through the blogosphere and was picked up by mainstream media.

When Howard Dean was making his bid for the Democratic presidential nomination, he shocked the political world by raising tremendous amounts of revenue through a grassroots Internet campaign. The word spread through the blogosphere at the speed of light and thousands of small donations streamed in. Once again, the power of the blogosphere's social networking capacity was demonstrated for all who cared to pay attention.

A quick Internet search will reveal conservative blogs, liberal blogs, moderate blogs, libertarian blogs, and even independent blogs. Bloggers of every political persuasion have found their public voice and blog away for all who will listen.

Everything from motherhood to politics can be impacted by blogging, but how does this trend impact educational leadership and why should the leader of the district or school administrator consider blogging?

WHY LEADERS SHOULD CONSIDER BLOGGING

In the current political arena that the educational leader operates in, it has become very important to be able to communicate with the public quickly and efficiently. The modern day leader with a blog and an active blog readership has developed one more tool to use in the overall communication plan for the school building or school district. There are a number of reasons why leaders should consider blogging.

If You Can't Beat 'Em—Join 'Em!

In the current world we live in, if the educational leader doesn't blog, then it is just a matter of time before others will blog about them. In many communities across the country, the superintendent of schools and the school principal are the best known public figures in the community. In small communities without a mayor or other elected official, the educational leader may be viewed as the most visible public figure. People in the community now expect them to have a public persona and to present a professional and transparent face to the community.

In today's world, blogging provides a ready-made public forum. I maintain that since you can't beat 'em, you might as well join 'em. I once received an e-mail from a patron on the East Coast who wanted me to see her blog site. I clicked on the hyperlink she provided in her e-mail and was surprised to find a blog site solely dedicated to an attempt to fire the superintendent of her school district. Each day she would blog to the community an ongoing attack on the superintendent's philosophies and practices. In this case she was seeking to influence the school board through public pressure to push for a change in leadership.

In another situation a superintendent was being dismissed by the school board. Supporters of the superintendent created a blog site for the express purpose of bashing the school board members in an attempt to save the superintendent. In both of these cases, the individuals involved turned to the Internet and blogging software to create a public forum for expressing their views. As you can very well imagine, the emotions on both sides were running high.

The old school mantra was, "Never argue with those who buy their ink by the barrel!" I maintain that the new mantra is, "Everyone has a barrel of ink so you better have one too."

Connecting with the Community—Old School

The educational leader who connected with the community in old school style was usually known for hanging out at the Friday night ball games and chatting up the crowd. They attended fish fries and chili suppers and did most of their communicating face-to-face. While attending these events is still a modern expectation in most school communities, the savvy school leader has realized that this crowd does not represent the entire community. Being physically present is not always possible for either the patrons or the school administrator.

Technology-minded school leaders are supplementing their old school political presence with a new school tool called the blog. When the leader has established a regular Internet presence, a much wider audience is cultivated. This audience is often a much more diverse community then those reached in traditional school audiences.

Connecting with the Community—New School

Blogging provides a forum to reach patrons who may be unreachable in conventional forums. The aging baby boomer population has created a scenario where it is likely that most of the power brokers and tax payers in the local community no longer have children or grandchildren in the school or district where they reside. Our highly mobile society has resulted in many retired folks who live in the community without any personal ties to individuals in the local school district. These folks may never get to know the school leader or the issues that plague their school system, at least through the conventional forums that school leaders have typically relied on. It is wise to remember that these individuals often control the tax levies and bond issues that often are the life's blood for many school communities. How do you keep them connected to the school and district?

As a former superintendent with an active blog readership, I found it interesting that a few of my most frequent blog readers and personal supporters were retired individuals in the community that I would cross paths with in the local fitness center. These individuals had no family in the local area, but had chosen to retire on one of the local tourist lakes popular in the region. These folks would chat frequently with me while jogging on the treadmills. The topics often gravitated to a subject I had blogged about that week. These individuals had no family members in the school district but were significant taxpayers in the community. Their only sources of information about schools were through the newspaper and the blog.

One frequent mistake that school leaders make is assuming that the patrons they see at traditional school events actually represent the entire community. It doesn't take long as a blogging school leader to recognize that there are multiple voices and multiple views on virtually every issue. Leaders who allow patrons to leave comments on their daily blogs will soon recognize the wide diversity of opinion that exists within any community.

As the baby boomers retire, their interest in schools is likely to shift towards fiscal issues and their own property tax burden. This means that to get public support for school bond issues and tax levies, superintendents and school boards will need to use every possible means to reach these individuals and to educate them about the issues facing the schools. The new school superintendent with a blogging audience may be able to provide this information on an ongoing basis to individuals who may not normally be connected to the school.

Blogging is just one tool in the tech-savvy superintendent's communication tool kit. Other methods of communicating, whether old school or new school, are still valuable and even necessary. The successful school leader will utilize a variety of strategies in an overall communication plan.

The New Media

With the rise in Internet accessibility and access to daily news online, many newspapers have found their readership dwindling. In order to counteract this trend, many newspapers have begun to publish online newspapers and blogs as the public begins a shift to online forums to read their news.

With this shift, the reading public has developed an appetite for current "just-in-time" news. The newspaper with its printing deadlines and slow turnaround time has found itself on the outside looking in. People who want current news, updated continually, will turn to the Internet or cable television for their news.

The tech-savvy superintendent will recognize that a daily blog will provide the public with a sense of current news from the school district. Because it takes no more than a mouse click, the Internet news user will find it quite simple to stop by the school district blog site to see what's new. The trick is to provide them a reason for stopping by your site. With the short attention spans of today's readers, you will only have a few seconds to catch their attention. If they stop by your site more than a few times and find little of interest, they are less likely to return.

We have mentioned how blogs got started and what they could mean for the modern school leader. Chapter two will review the advantages to blogging and what several experts have to say about what blogging can do for you.

2

ADVANTAGES OF BLOGGING

A BLOGGER IS BORN

I rocked back in my office chair and kneaded the muscle knotting up my left shoulder. I glanced at the clock and realized it was getting late. I rocked forward and stared once again at my computer screen. I contemplated the little blinking cursor poised over the "Publish Blog Now" button. I rubbed my tired eyes and contemplated the public persona I was about to share with the entire world. Was I ready for this? The technical side of starting my own blog site had only taken ten minutes or so, but becoming a real blogger seemed like a much bigger step.

My palms began to sweat, as I visualized people from anywhere in the world stumbling into my blog site and reading what I posted. I pictured hundreds of people all over the local community reading my commentary and taking exception to it in the privacy of their own living rooms. Blogging about music or sports seemed like one thing, but starting a blog about your own profession where everyone in the community thinks they know how to do your job better than you do, seemed like something else entirely. I thought of the book I had just read on blogging and how it may have changed the political landscape forever.

I sighed and poised with my index finger over the enter key and stared at the blinking cursor again. With trepidation I pressed the keyboard key and a blogger was born.

Being a blogger may take awhile but starting your own blog site is a simple way to develop your own web presence.

BLOGS ARE AN EASY WAY TO HAVE YOUR OWN WEBSITE

By using the free blogging software that is available online, you can develop your own website very quickly. For someone that just wants to get a simple website up with the potential for public interaction controlled by the blog author, the blog may be the easiest way to get started.

BLOGS ARE EASY TO CREATE

Blogs can be very simple to create. By simply following the step-by-step directions on most of the free blog software websites, a person can be up and running within minutes. In the early days of blogging, knowledge of Hyper Text Markup Language (HTML) was a prerequisite. Today a new blogger can follow the simple menu-driven directions, and be up and blogging in minutes without any formal training or experience in website design.

BLOGS ARE EASY TO MAINTAIN

Most blog maintenance simply involves reading the blog every day and posting new content. If the blog author has the public comment features turned on, it may take a little more effort to maintain the blog due to the public interaction. Monitoring the blog for public profanity, slanderous or defamatory comments, or spammers is a daily maintenance issue. Many bloggers give access rights to other people so that more than one person can maintain the site. As a blogging superintendent I often had other people monitor the site so that we could delete inappropriate comments as needed. I occasionally would get a call in the evening from someone who wanted to alert me to a rude comment on the blog. With a few mouse clicks we could delete or block comments as necessary.

BLOGS ARE SEARCH ENGINE FRIENDLY

Because blogs are updated constantly, they tend to move up the priority list on the major search engines found on the Internet. Static websites that are not updated or accessed regularly will tend to get less daily traffic, which moves them down the list. Some search engines, like Technorati, search only blogs instead of all websites. In most cases, search engines tend to treat blogs very kindly due to their frequent traffic and regular updates. This means that your blog may surface near the top of the search lists if it gets frequent traffic.

MANY BLOG HOSTS ARE FREE

With the explosion of Internet activity, many sites are now hosting blog space for free. These sites are able to provide this space for free because so many blog sites are allowing blog ads on their webpages. The advertising sales allow the blog software to be free to users. While many of these free blog sites will offer enhanced features for a price, the basic blog necessities are often provided for free, even if you choose not to allow ads on your site. When I was actively blogging as a school superintendent I would occasionally call and line up local advertisers for the blog site and simply ask them to make a donation to the local school on the behalf of needy children. By offering this to local businesses, they can have a local online presence. With a simple donation they could benefit the local community and your blog site could avoid the national advertising you see on most blog sites.

In addition to blogs being easy, another benefit is that as the author of the blog, you control the message.

YOU CONTROL YOUR MESSAGE

One of the greatest advantages to blogging as a school leader is that you control the central message to your site. There is no risk of being misquoted. If it comes out wrong, it's entirely your fault. The school leader doesn't have to be entirely dependent on other people to get their message out. Of course this isn't for the faint of heart because there is no one else to blame!

While the central message is controlled through the regular postings on the blog site, you don't always control the public's reaction to those postings unless you choose to moderate the comments. The superintendent may control even the responses by requiring all comments to be approved before posting or by not allowing any comments. These decisions are entirely under the control of the blog moderator. Of course, like most things, there are benefits and drawbacks to both options.

Despite the draw backs, which we will discuss later, the primary benefit to blogging is that you have a free and open forum for expressing your opinions without having to work through other media outlets. When working with other media outlets you are at the mercy of the daily news cycle and the events of the day. Nothing can be more discouraging to an educational leader than to work very hard getting exposure for a particular program or issue only to see your article relegated to the back pages of the paper, pushed off the front page by a local fire at the drugstore. When you have active daily readership for your blog, nothing pushes you off the front page. You are the front page.

Another benefit to blogging is that it provides you a regular forum for responding to traditional media.

YOU CAN RESPOND TO TRADITIONAL MEDIA

A commonly expressed frustration of school leaders is the occasional occurrence of inaccurate or misleading stories printed in the local newspapers. The leader with a regular blog and a dependable readership can instantly make a correction or respond to inaccurate reports published in traditional media outlets. The normal response of the school leader is to fire off a letter to the editor of the paper, explaining or correcting the perceived inaccuracies. The problem is that by the time the letter to the editor is published, readers may not remember the original article that prompted it. Or perhaps they never got around to reading it at all.

With many newspapers now publishing online versions of their newspapers and archiving them, the tech savvy superintendent can write a response to the article on the blog and then hyperlink to the original article so the public can refer to it. In addition, the superintendent can write a traditional letter to the editor for the hard copy version of the newspaper and then refer the public to the blog site for a complete review of the story.

Another benefit to blogging is that your message is archived and is therefore retrievable. Patrons do not have a particular time window when they have to be watching or listening in order to get the message.

THE MESSAGE IS ASYNCHRONOUS—YOU DON'T HAVE TO BE PRESENT TO WIN!

A great advantage to the technology of blogging is that it is asynchronous, meaning that things don't have to happen in chronological order. In our busy world, patrons are on the go continually. With so many activities and events going on, school supporters are not always able to attend the school board meetings and conventional communication events that occur in real time. The local newspaper may already be lining the bottom of the bird cage by the time they get around to trying to read the article explaining the new building project. Accessing announcements and daily postings through a blog site allows patrons to keep up on such issues.

The archiving software features even allow the patrons to instantly search your entire blog site by entering search terms for the topics they are interested in. Any postings you have made on this topic will instantly pop up, allowing the busy reader to determine what your take was on this issue. This asynchronous feature is very useful in today's busy world. Another bonus is that searching the archives is a lot less messy than dragging the newspaper out from the bottom of the bird cage!

Another benefit of blogging is that it actually increases your school district's coverage with the traditional local media outlets.

IT INCREASES COVERAGE IN TRADITIONAL MEDIA

Perhaps one of the most unusual and counterintuitive things I found as a blogging superintendent is that the traditional media outlets actually read my blog and contacted me more frequently for interviews. My first thought when I started blogging was that newspapers would feel threatened and that journalists would not seek out my opinion as often because I would have my own forum for releasing information. I found the opposite to be true. I found that numerous journalists, especially those who cover educational issues exclusively, were frequent blog readers who scoured the web weekly looking for potential story ideas. They frequently called seeking my opinion on a variety of issues. This also increased the positive exposure of the school district in traditional media outlets. It wasn't just the local media either. I actually had major market newspapers start calling me for quotes and opinions on educational issues simply because the newspaper education editor was a weekly reader of my blog.

On one occasion I blogged about high school dropout rates and linked to a story in the *Indianapolis Star* on the same topic. The *Star* had run a series on graduation rates and dropout rates and I had questioned their calculation methods. While I thought it was true that current high school graduation rates were inflated across the country, I still thought the *Indianapolis Star*'s calculations on dropouts were flawed. I blogged about the topic and a few days later the *Indianapolis Star*'s education editor responded to my posts by commenting on the blog. This is an example of how blogging can elevate the discussion and bring into the fray the main players and stakeholders.

Another benefit to blogging is that it builds a sense of community with your readers.

IT BUILDS A SENSE OF COMMUNITY

The online environment builds a sense of community among regular readers. The wise leader never overlooks an opportunity for community building. One very important part of this blogging network is that it often brings a sense of community to people that are not always in the normal network of school events. This concept hit home forcibly one week when a patron sent me a private e-mail acknowledging how much she felt a part of the school system since reading my blog. In the e-mail she left her name. After inquiring with our principals I learned a little more about her. She was a parent with two special needs children, living in a small trailer park. She had very little formal education and minimal family income, but she had an Internet connection and she used it to stay on top of school activities and issues. In her e-mail she acknowledged that she felt too intimidated to call or stop by the office but she felt brave enough to talk to the superintendent through anonymous blog comments and e-mail.

Here is the text of her e-mail.

Good afternoon Dr. Mark Stock,

My name is Ruth Anne (name changed to protect her confidentiality). *I have not met you. Since The Wawascene (my blog site) is easily accessible I felt I could share my experience on a recent topic. I have a daughter with Autism and she attends your school. This is in reference to your blog post, "The Day I Became Convinced that Special Needs Students aren't the Only Ones Benefitting from being Included" story in The Wawascene. I have, and thank God my daughter has, experienced this spectacular occurrence since preschool. I have shed many tears of amazement over the fact that there are those peers that have this unselfish, giving, accepting way about them. I have seen it happen many times over. In fact one little girl has been purposely put into my daughter's home room each year. This is usually in agreement at the IEP meetings. I have personally spoken to her parents and they are totally aware of this fact and they feel good about them being together. This little girl has helped my daughter in so many ways. The little girl began doing this without any assistance or pressure to help my daughter. She does this purely on her own desires to be there when needed as her peer helper with no questions asked. Our experience with children like this little girl is not the only one that has touched this Special Needs parent's heart.*

By the way, your story touched me the same as I get touched by these giving children every day. Tears of unexplainable amazement. These are future loving parents, nurses, doctors, teachers, counselors and so on.

I felt a need to put this on your blog but it is just too personal to me and I felt it was appropriate to email.

Thank you for your time and have a great day!

Ruth Anne

Letters like these are what allow administrators to keep plugging away at their jobs in the midst of deteriorating public support. Yet in the trenches with the parents and students, success stories like these abound.

This is the blog post that I put up on "The Wawascene" that prompted Ruth Anne's personal e-mail to me.

The day I became convinced that special needs students weren't the only ones benefitting from being included.
The Setting
It was the fall of 1984. I had just moved to Indiana from Ohio to take a 6th grade teaching position. One of the differences I noticed at Washington Elementary in Warsaw, Indiana was the number of special needs students in the school due to the centralized special education cooperative. There were students from Whitko, Wawasee, and Tippecanoe Valley all attending our school. The school I came from in Ohio did not have any special needs students with the exception of Learning Disabled (LD) students.

The Story

The sun was shining brightly, reflecting off the dark asphalt of the outdoor basketball courts outside Washington Elementary. Several hundred students stood silently in straight lines, hands at their sides, squinting into the sun and watching their teachers for a silent signal to re-enter the school after a fire drill practice.

Suddenly a strange noise came from the playground. The students silently turned to look. A little handicapped boy with Down's Syndrome came skipping and prancing off the playground, dancing and singing loudly to a tune only he could hear. A fire drill wasn't going to interfere with his day!

I immediately whipped around and gave everyone the "evil teacher eye." You know, that stern piercing look that all teachers learn fast or they don't survive long. I expected rude laughter and some version of poking fun at him. Young teenagers can be cruel and unmerciful at times when it comes to picking on others and I expected this to be ugly.

The incident I witnessed following this exchange has forever convinced me that general education students learn a lot from going to school with students with diverse needs.

My class watched the little boy with understanding expressions and quiet, patient smiles. Several whispered his name, "Hi Jon!" Others covertly snuck their hands out and gave him a quiet "high five" as he danced by. No snide remarks. No secret whispers. No knowing grins.

I glanced at every student and studied their expressions carefully. I could see only signs of friendliness. I studied them carefully again, this time looking for pity in their eyes. Still—only friendliness.

It was awhile later before I truly understood how this could be. You see, Washington Elementary 6th grade students were friends with Jon. They routinely gave up their recesses and went to the special needs classrooms to help tutor and befriend the students. They didn't poke fun at Jon because they knew him. They didn't pity him because they knew he could do a lot of things. They were Jon's friends.

While there are certainly challenges when we include special needs students in regular education, let's not forget that special education students aren't the only ones who benefit.

This blog post, and the parent e-mail that followed it, emphasized once again, that the community is full of people who care that often feel too intimidated to make their opinions known in more traditional ways. The sense of community that can occur in online environments can be very powerful.

Think about the relationships you are building behind the scenes when hundreds and even thousands of people are reading your postings and daily musings. If done well, these readers will soon develop a feel for who you are and what you represent through these daily postings.

There are many benefits to blogging that can be advantageous to the educational leader and the school district. The following list outlines a variety of ways that school leaders can use blogging to their advantage.

SPREAD THE NEWS

Perhaps the simplest and most common way of getting started on accessing the benefits of blogging is to use the blog site as an electronic newsletter. The public relations savvy leader will take all items typically released in a traditional newsletter and simply cut-and-paste the items, including pictures, onto the local blog site. This is a quick, cheap, and easy way to release a variety of information. As a blogging superintendent I would frequently announce the results of various athletic events or post the decisions from the previous evening's school board meetings. In communities with active local media and daily newspapers, it can be even simpler.

When local newspapers have carried online coverage of school events, the blogging school leader can simply hyperlink to the articles that are already on the web and include any talking points or clarifications. In this way the blogging school leader can spread the news even when they don't post the actual news themselves.

In addition to spreading the good news, the blog can be used as method of communicating during an emergency.

COMMUNICATING DURING AN EMERGENCY

One of the most helpful ways of communicating important information during an emergency is to use the local blog site. Snow delays, snow cancellations, power outages, bomb threats and other emergencies can be chronicled online through the leader's blog site. The advantage to using the blog site to update the public in an emergency situation is that the information is available online as soon as the patron accesses the site. With traditional media such as radio and television, the patron is not always able to access the information immediately. Another advantage is that it can free up the busy phone lines by taking away at least some of the phone traffic.

One year when I was a superintendent, we had a lockdown procedure in progress at a local school due to a potential gun threat. When patrons saw the lockdown procedure go into effect they immediately began to call the local school. The school personnel referred them immediately to my blog site. On my blog I detailed the chronology of the event and indicated that everyone was safe and that as soon as the situation was resolved I would post immediately. We had thousands of hits on the site during the short crisis. The local patrons knew where to go to get the most current and accurate information. Patrons posted comments thanking me for publishing the information and keeping them informed.

Here is the post that went up on "The Wawascene" blog site at 11:55 AM.

Quick Update on Milford School

We took a few calls regarding Milford School being in "lock-down" so I thought I would post the real story this morning to squelch any wild rumors.

Milford School went into "lock-down" this morning as students were entering the school. A student had allegedly made a "threat" and left the building indicating they might return shortly. The school immediately went into lock-down procedure as they are trained to do. The police immediately went to the home and took the child into custody.

The school came out of lock-down and started their normal schedule. Thank you to the school administrators, teachers, employees and students for handling the situation quickly and professionally.

Thank you to the parent who called here immediately to get the real story.

Posted by Dr. Mark J. Stock at 11:55 AM

Several parent comments on the blog post regarding the Milford lockdown demonstrate clearly how there are a variety of opinions and voices within your community.

Here are two different parent comments regarding the same post and situation.

Anonymous said . . .

I came to school to help in my daughter's class. I saw the police officer when I came in. When I was leaving the school NOT even the office staff would tell me what happened. I am outraged at how NO ONE will tell me what happened in my CHILDREN'S school. I was told to read your blog. Now that isn't right. I should be told what is going on. I have a daughter in the MS, and it just scares me to see that something could have happened and I wouldn't be made aware of. I think the way that the school dealt with notifying parents needs to be redone. I guess if I want to find out what's going on, I will turn on the NEWS and HEAR it from them first.
9/19/2006

Anonymous said . . .

Dr. Stock: Thank you for promptly posting this and providing a reliable source of information. Our children told us something happened and, as parents, we are glad that you maintain a forum of this nature for a convenient and accurate way to see what is going on. We understand why you cannot have multiple people answering questions to the public. Keeping sources to a minimal number and limiting it to people of authority, maintains accuracy and reduces rumors.
9/19/2006

Another day we had a bus accident in which the driver of another vehicle was killed. Upon arrival at the hospital, I immediately accessed a computer from the hospital waiting area and blogged an update, indicating that all the students were currently safe and in good condition. I proceeded to announce the procedures we would use for releasing students to their parents from the hospital. Blogging the incident "live" from the hospital gave the blog site legitimacy as a forum for current and accurate information. It also reinforced the importance of this forum and brought new readers to the site.

When I arrived at the accident site, most of the students had already text-messaged their family, called them on their cell phones, and even e-mailed pictures immediately to their friends right from their cell phones. I arrived at the site within minutes and there were already a handful of parents outside the buses waiting. Students and parents are now accustomed to this type of instantaneous communication. Whenever the school leader can provide this level of communication as well, it is generally appreciated by most of the community.

Here is the post I put on "The Wawascene" to inform the public.

This Morning's Bus Accident Update
Some of you know by now that there was bus accident around 7:30 AM this morning. Bus 16 was traveling on the north side of Dewart Lake and was struck head on by a small car. Everyone appears to be ok but due to the severity of the collision we transported all the students to Kosciusko Hospital just to be sure. Administrators met the parents at the hospital to explain the situation. After checking all the students over carefully, KCH released some to their parents and others were transported back to the school. KCH provided a breakfast and snacks for students after they were officially released.

We wish to thank the EMS workers and volunteers as well as law enforcement officials for their professional and speedy response.

Thanks to the hospital for allowing me to blog this directly from the hospital computers.

Posted by Superintendent, Dr. Mark J. Stock at 12:07

Here is another example of communicating in an emergency. This excerpt comes from the blog, "The Plymouth Truth." This is the blog of the superintendent of the Plymouth Community School Corporation in Plymouth, Indiana.

Monday, May 12, 2008
Blog Bits
Plymouth High School
Bomb Threat Case Resolved
The administration of Plymouth High School reports that the investigation of last week's bomb threat has been completed with a receipt of an admission of guilt from a high school student. The PHS administration wishes to thank all those involved in the investigation including the Plymouth Police Force, students, parents, and other school and community stakeholders who provided valuable information in the process. At this time, the school will work in conjunction with the Plymouth Police Department to ensure that due process is followed.
posted by Dan and Damon @ 5/12/2008 10:52:00 AM

In addition to communicating in an emergency, a blog site can be used to monitor ongoing events or issues.

MONITORING ONGOING EVENTS

Using the blog is a great way to monitor progress of a project or event that is ongoing in your school district. A former superintendent and colleague of mine, Dr. John Hill, used his blog "The Plymouth Truth" to report regular progress on building construction projects. Weekly construction updates, including reports on road closures and other issues, kept readers informed of the project's development. Any ongoing event that requires a regular updating of information for the public may provide good blogging material.

Here is an example of monitoring an ongoing construction project.

Wednesday, August 30, 2006
Blog Bits
Construction Updates
The rain has slowed construction on the Elm Street extension. The installation of curbs, gutters, and sidewalks is now pushed back one to two weeks depending on the weather, Paving of the street and remaining parking lot will take place shortly thereafter. The carpet is installed in the media center. Contractors will begin working on the casework next week, The carpet will be installed in the music room tomorrow.

The rehabilitation of the Soccerplex will be completed as soon as weather permits.

At PHS, the gymnasium will be available as soon as the railings are installed. This is scheduled to take place next week.

Thank You.

Thank you for your patience during construction.

Bus Route Adjustments
  The transportation department will continue to make adjustments in routes to balance busloads. If you have any questions, please contact Rick Scott (936-3115).
  The full day kindergarten and ENL mid-day routes will begin next Wednesday.
  posted by Dan and Damon @ 8/30/2006 08:21:00 PM 4 comments

One of the most practical examples of monitoring ongoing events with a blog is chronicling the ongoing weather issues that plague some districts. On mornings where snowfall and icy conditions threatened school closings, my blog site traffic would increase substantially. It was not uncommon for my blog site to have five thousand hits before 6:00 AM on snowy days. On these high traffic days it is important for the educational leader to use these opportunities to educate the public on other issues of importance to the school district. I routinely saved important, but not necessarily time-sensitive, postings in draft mode and held them until high Internet traffic was occurring. By releasing these posts when the readership is high and Internet traffic is at a maximum, the educational leader is maximizing their opportunities to share important information or ideas with the public.

One of the most memorable high traffic days I ever experienced occurred on such a day. It was a snowy, nasty winter morning and the site traffic was already high as community members and parents monitored the site to see if the two-hour snow delay would be changed to a cancellation due to the deteriorating weather conditions. When I didn't announce a cancellation, the comments turned angry. A few patrons considered the decision to have school to be a mistake, and that is putting it mildly! When they took a few pot shots at me on the comment section of the blog, a few more patrons came on to defend me. One of the defenders decided to make a snide comment about "stay-at-home" moms whining on the Internet and told them to "go bake some cookies or something." It immediately turned into the *Jerry Springer Show* and the patrons were soon throwing mud at each other.

While it was mostly comical, I eventually shut off the comments at 119 and froze it so that more comments couldn't be made on that posting. There were over seventy-one thousand hits on the site that day and it was the talk of town everywhere I went. As I walked the halls of the high school, the students would smile knowingly at me and it was clear that even the students were reading the blog and talking about it. The critical point here is that it takes a few of these days to drive community awareness of the blog to higher levels. Days like that are not common occurrences for the blogging leader, and they are usually uncomfortable. But one unusual side effect is that they tend to drive traffic to higher levels and obtain new readers. Most school leaders shy away from such perceived negativity, but for the most part issues like this are harmless and do bring about more interest in the blog site.

After watching the rough and tumble interaction on the blog site regarding the weather decisions in the district, I received the following e-mail from a parent. Once again, this e-mail shows the empathy that can develop among members of the public when they recognize the difficulty of your position.

Dr. Stock,

I want to thank you for your concern for our children this week, I feel the remarks you have been getting are so uncalled for! I personally would not want your job for anything—you can't win—no matter what!! You have been wonderful in considering the weather, temperatures and safety of the kids! Last week when you took the heat for your "Blew It" post, my husband had gone to work early and said he had no trouble—the bad weather set in after the normal time for delay! I just wanted you to know that I read your Blog—and enjoy the different tidbits you add to it! Thank you again for your great concerns this week.

Sue S.

Blogging is a contact sport and those with thin skin probably won't appreciate it. My personal experience is that this type of day is often caused by students posing as adults and simply enjoying the spectacle of watching adults weigh into the fray and take their comments seriously.

After this particular incident occurred, an employee stopped by to let me know that their own high school age children were observed clustered around the computer with their friends, posing as adults and posting comments.

In almost every case where a major outbreak of this type of negativity occurred, it happened on a snowy day where there was a large increase in the number of students monitoring the blog site with the hopes that school would be canceled or delayed. The solution to this temporary issue was to shut off comments on the postings regarding weather delays. However, the positive side to what happened is that it brought thousands of new readers to the site as it became the talk of the town.

Despite the tendency for blog comments to turn negative, there are just enough e-mails like the next one show to how the general public feels about it.

From: JD
Sent: Tuesday, February 06
To: mstock@wawasee.k12.in.us
Subject: School Delays—not a complaint
   I really appreciate the early notices of delays and cancellations. I would not like to be in your position. You are doing a wonderful job. You work just as hard as the next person. I normally just check the Wawascene Blog site for delays or cancellations. I watch the morning news, have the radio on and also check the WSBT website.
   My oldest sister is a teacher in South Bend and they don't have a school blog.
   I just wanted to say a big thank you.
   Have a wonderful day.
   J.D.

Another way to use a blog is to use it for political purposes. Education is essentially a political process, which means the educational leader's job often involves educating the public about how legislation would affect the local school district.

BEING AN ACTIVIST

Every school leader knows that being an advocate and an activist for public education is a critical part of the leadership function. Being politically active is not only a professional obligation but in many communities it is a school board expectation of the leader. There are traditional ways that leaders can be involved in the political function through professional associations at the state and national level. However, there is a growing need for community activism at the grassroots level.

Think about the potential impact on the political scene if every superintendent in America had an active and growing readership on their local blog site. In many small communities across America the local superintendent is the closest thing they have to a local political figure. Imagine how quickly important messages could be distributed when a legislative bill in the state or local government was introduced. On my blog site I placed a small "sticker" on the sidebar that allowed a patron to e-mail their legislator. This "sticker" was a small piece of JavaScript code that permitted the patron to type in their zip code and then their street address. This not only gave them the names and contact information for all their state and national political representatives, but it gave them a pop up screen allowing them to instantly type an e-mail message that went to their legislator. This made political activism on educational issues as simple as a few mouse clicks and typing a short e-mail message.

Here is an example of a blog post meant to educate the local community about a potential bill winding its way through the legislative process. Notice that I provided a hyperlink to the actual bill so that patrons can read it for themselves. Also notice the references to the legislative sticker on the sidebar so that patrons can e-mail their legislators directly from the blog site.

What do you think of this proposed law?

Here is a bill that would take away the Indiana driver's license of any minor that was caught smoking.

Digest of Introduced Bill

Driver's license suspension for minors who smoke. Permits a court to order a: (1) one year suspension of a driver's license of; or (2) a six month delay in the issuance of a driver's license to; a minor who violates tobacco laws.

Authored by Senator(s) Boots

Hmmm! Is this a good idea or not?

If you have an opinion—just put your zip code in the blue box labeled "Write your legislators." Enter your address and your legislator's email address will come up. You can let your representatives know what you think.

Here is a list of all proposed legislation. Scroll through them and see what your legislators are up to!

Posted by Superintendent, Dr. Mark J. Stock at 1:16 PM 10 comments

Labels: Legislation

One state legislator told me that he stacked up all the form letters from the lobbyists and their associations into one big pile and then considered them as one letter. Then he looked at all the private e-mails and personal letters and stacked them up and considered them individually. What he was trying to tell me was that he put great importance on the opinion of separate individuals that were part of his constituency. Think about how powerful it would be if even one-third of your blog readers sent their legislator an e-mail telling them what they thought about a piece of legislation. The grassroots activism on educational issues would increase tremendously. While legislators are accustomed to hearing from paid professional lobbyists, they are not often accustomed to hearing from individual patrons.

In addition to using the blog as a political tool, the savvy superintendent will use their blog site as a marketing and public relations tool.

MARKETING AND PR

School leaders are increasingly aware of the need for marketing our schools. The privatization of schools and the increase of public and private school choice have resulted in a heightened awareness of the need to put forth the good news about public schools. A blogging school leader with a faithful readership will find regular opportunities to share the positive aspects of the school district. The tech savvy school leader can share video clips from the ball game and post graphs and audio blogs explaining the latest school district test scores released in the newspapers. All these can be integrated into a multimedia look and feel that will utilize the strengths of the Internet.

People in the community want to be part of what's happening. When they explain at the office how they heard about it on the school superintendent's blog site, it will slowly spread the readership around the community. Schools have not followed the traditional business model of marketing their products. Nonetheless, schools have a long track record of successfully promoting schools. The successful school leader will continue to use traditional public relations methods but will also use the blog site and other modern tools as well. All press releases or newspaper articles may be used as blog material as well as promoted in the traditional media outlets.

Another way of using the blog is to use it as a forum for helping the community get to know you.

GETTING TO KNOW YOU

How does the person who has never met you, get to know you? With the Internet it is now possible to feel a sense of connection to people you have never physically met. I would often receive private e-mails from patrons expressing gratitude for the blog and the information I provided. They inevitably would add a comment about how much sympathy they had for my difficult job. The greater community generally recognizes how much courage it takes to maintain a public presence on a blog site. They will often feel an emotional connection to you even when they haven't personally met you. Your authenticity will show through your postings and they will catch glimpses of the person behind the position.

I was told once by Griff Wigley, a blog consultant, that the reason my blog site was working was that I didn't write to the people in superintendent memo mode. For example, on Fridays I ran a regular feature called "Friday's Funnies" where I detailed funny stories about kids. I had many readers tell me that they usually logged onto the site on Fridays just to get a chuckle for the day. And while they were there of course, they scrolled down through the postings to see what else I was rambling about that week. Showing a sense of humor is a critical part of letting the community know who you are.

Here is an example of showing a sense of humor. The idea for this post came to me one morning when I opened a letter from the federal government talking about No Child Left Behind (NCLB). It was full of so much jargon and acronyms it was hard to tell if it was written in English. If you have ever read a long memorandum from the federal government you will know exactly why this is humorous.

Alphabet Soup
I received a 5 page letter today from the government explaining new monitoring procedures for No Child Left Behind. This is what it said in abbreviated form.

The NCLB legislation requires the IDOE to monitor each LEA in reviewing the SWP and SIP's as soon as EIS has it up and running.

There don't you feel enlightened!

It's a good thing I was mostly paying attention in kindergarten and learned my letters!

Have a good day. EIEIO
Posted by Superintendent, Dr. Mark J. Stock at 10:38 AM

Another way of connecting personally with your readers is to tell about a vacation you went on or tell about your hobbies and what you do for fun. This promotes a sense of humanness and is part of what helps us see our leaders as approachable and normal. On occasion I would refer to my children and use examples of routine family life that would help readers feel like they knew a little more about me.

One of the most popular posts I ever ran was my annual Mother's Day Tribute. This usually got a few responses from patrons, usually mothers, who were touched by the story. Here is the annual Mother's Day tribute I posted on my blog followed by a patron comment that was posted.

Mother's Day Tribute
I post this each year in honor of upcoming Mother's Day.

My mother passed away several years ago, leaving behind a wonderful tribute and family legacy. On Mothers' Day it seems appropriate to remember her.

When I was 8 years old, my father passed away after losing a battle with a brain tumor, leaving my mother a widow at age 32 with three children under the age of 8. Mother had been a stay-at-home mom and dad was an airline mechanic for Delta Airlines. Mom did not have marketable job training that would provide a living wage. Unsure of what to do, she moved our family from Michigan to Ohio to be closer to her parents. She bought a small home and enrolled in college at Wright State University in Fairborn, Ohio. Her goal was to become a classroom teacher. My brother, sister and I can still hear her late into the night, studying by reading out loud to herself. I can hardly imagine the stress and workload of a single, widowed mother of three young children taking a full load of classes at the university. Mother graduated with academic honors in four years and got her first full-time employment as a third grade teacher at the age of 38. I can still remember how excited us children were that mom could finally afford to buy soda-pop for a family treat.

From my earliest memory, I knew that I was going to go to college because mom did, yet the greatest gift my mother left us was her spiritual example. She overcame all obstacles placed before her, and although her life could never have been described as easy, she was satisfied in what life had brought. She never complained, but set a solid example of honesty, integrity and work ethic that has remained a legacy, not only to her children but also to all who knew her. She never remarried, but chose to dedicate her life to God, her family and her elementary school students.

From her example of going to college and working hard, her three children continued their education as well. In her last few years while fighting cancer, she helped me finish my doctoral dissertation by entering all my data into spreadsheets. My sister completed her college degree and passed her CPA exams and my brother went back to school to finish an MBA.

The research says that one of the highest correlations for educational achievement for any individual is found by tracking the educational degree of the mother. It certainly seems true for our family. Here in America, the greatest land of opportunity the world has ever known, let us be thankful for caring and dedicated mothers who model the values and work ethic that made America great. Especially those single mothers who must play many roles for their children. Mothers, take courage, your children will not forget the legacy you leave them. May it be a positive one.
Posted by Superintendent, Dr. Mark J. Stock at 6:49 PM

Following this post were these four comments from readers. Anonymous said . . .

Thanks for an inspiring story! I'm sure your mother would be proud of you! I agree that we can be an example for our children and as a school we can help parents out there to be a positive example for theirs. While your mother was an amazing woman with self-motivation, she also must have relied on the support from others. Many of our parents don't have support or positive role models. We can help be the stepping stone for parents in our community as well. Thanks for a great message!
5/09/2005

Anonymous said . . .

What a wonderful way to honor thy mother! It has been said "we never know how much we have, until it is gone". By reading your touching words, it is evident you knew how precious life was for your family, a true gift from God. Cherish the memories and continue to live on in the true spirit of family. All children are beautiful in their own way, encouraging a child to never stop learning in life is what makes our world so bright.
Thank you for sharing and for leading our youth.
5/09/2005

Anonymous said . . .

Mark—So inspiring and so true! Thank you!
5/10/2005

Anonymous said . . .

Your story inspired me as an educator and as a mother. Thanks for
sharing.
5/10/2005

It is through posts like these that your constituents will get to know who you are. The essence of what you believe and what you stand for can shine through your postings and help people know you who have never met you in person. For a high profile educational leader this is of utmost importance. I do not believe it is possible to overestimate the potential benefits of this aspect of successful blogging.

In today's busy world, it is more difficult than ever to find the time to get to know other people. The Internet has helped fill a gap in this regard and has allowed people to connect through the web.

Another way to use the blog is to use it as a forum for educating the community about important issues.

EDUCATING THE COMMUNITY

Perhaps one of the most useful ways of using your blog site is to use it as a teaching tool. Educational leaders often find themselves making decisions that appear confusing at best and at worst hypocritical to local community members. The main reason is that the leaders often have information and knowledge that may not be readily available or apparent to the local patrons. The use of a blog site is an excellent way to inform and educate the public on matters of urgency or political importance.

The best method is to dole out the information in small doses in daily or weekly postings. This not only allows readers the opportunity to digest the information in small doses, but it also provides a method of reviewing the information over time without the appearance of being demeaning. Some very complex issues can be explained to the public very successfully through a blog.

I frequently blogged about the complexities of property taxes to our local patrons. Due to the large number of lakefront properties, our school district had some of the highest assessed property values in the state yet the school district's per pupil revenues were low. Explaining this disconnect to local patrons was always a challenge. Individuals would open their property tax bills and assume that the large increases were going to the local school district. Through blogging about this concept and explaining over and over again about the state's complicated school funding formula, I was able to take some of the mysteries out of this issue for our readers. Readers could then use the blog site's search feature to call up any articles or postings I had ever done related to property tax issues. This provided a sense of history and an archived review for newer readers.

The following postings and comments from the public will provide a sense of how a school leader might use a blog to educate the readership on fairly complex issues. There is probably nothing more complicated to the average citizen than how property taxes and school funding work. The following blog posts taken from "The Wawascene" describe how a specific piece of Indiana legislation could affect local schools and municipalities. Following the post is a series of comments made by readers, some fairly critical of me. Within these comments you find my own personal responses to their comments.

I have found that it is through this give and take response that trust and confidence in the school leader will grow. Notice the last comment made by a patron at the very end of this threaded discussion. Also notice that a number of the blog comments come from patrons who appear to be fairly knowledgeable but have very different views.

Sunday, February 11, 2007
"2% circuit breaker"—For some cities, towns and schools it blows a fuse!

Someone emailed me last week and wanted to know how Indiana's new law, coined the "2% circuit breaker" was going to affect the Wawasee school system. Evidently they had seen the TV coverage of the South Bend school system fretting about how this law could hurt them badly.

The "2% circuit breaker," passed by the Indiana General Assembly in 2006 is designed to cap property taxes at 2%. That sounds simple enough, right?

Yet, this law could have a devastating impact on some municipalities, towns, cities and schools but little or no impact on others. Here is how it works. To make the example simple, let's assume you had a home and property that was valued for property tax purposes at $100,000 and your total property tax exceeded $2,000. In this example the "2% circuit breaker" kicks in and then anything over that $2,000 is uncollectable and the taxing entities would not receive their portion of that money.

What if you live in a town that has a library tax? What if your town provides sewer service? Maybe they collect your garbage or plow your streets and pick up your leaves? These services are provided for those that live in the taxing area. But if your total property taxes including school taxes exceeds 2% (or in the $100,000 example—$2,000) then the taxing entities do not receive their portion over the $2,000 amount.

This seems a little weird to me. Just because you live outside these municipal areas doesn't necessarily mean you don't use such services. Maybe you pay for your own garbage pickup. When the private gravel drive to your subdivision is drifted in you may have to pay separately to have it plowed. You probably pay every year to have it scraped and potholes filled. Maybe you pay for septic tanks to be pumped and when the systems go bad you may pay privately to put in a new system. These items are not covered on the property tax rolls but that doesn't mean you don't have to use those services. I suppose the thinking is that at least you have a choice. I suppose so. You could let the garbage pile up at the roadside I guess! :-)

But, here are the real problems with the "2% circuit breaker:"

1. These towns, municipalities and schools already have their budgets set and services developed long before they are informed about how much revenue is not collected.
2. The Indiana General Assembly passed the law without solid information on how and who it would affect.
3. They did not pass any alternative revenue sources.

As far as Wawasee Schools is concerned, it does not appear to have too much of a direct effect. Wawasee School's tax rate is low enough that even adding all the other property taxes up inside the towns it should not have a major impact on our schools. But time will tell.

To see Wawasee's property tax rate and current ranking (Click here) then scroll down to "Delve deeper into data" and select "top 10 corporations," then select "tax rate (before CAGIT)" and you will see Wawasee ranked 292 of 293 school districts in Indiana. In other words, Wawasee's tax rate is among the lowest in the state.

Posted by Superintendent, Dr. Mark J. Stock at 9:48 PM 13 comments

Here are the comments made by readers following my blog post on property taxes and the 2% circuit breaker legislation in Indiana.

Anonymous said . . .

Maybe the 2% circuit breaker was not researched enough before implementation; however, families are losing homes due to high property taxes. At least this was an attempt to control these taxes which on av-

erage have risen 25% over the last few years while incomes have risen only 14% over the same time. Indiana is 6th in the nation in home foreclosure rates. The property tax system is in need of drastic reform! While it is not fair to short change schools, it is also not fair to tax a family out of their home! The system needs to be based on ability to pay (income taxes) or usage (sales taxes). Some will argue that these taxes are not as stable as property taxes. With this said, it is about time our gov's give attention to our incomes not just that of cities and towns, schools etc. Why are not cities and towns run like a business or for that matter like a household? That is, during good times one expands and invests. During lean times, yes this is difficult, one cuts back and does not implement that new program or buy that new piece of equipment. You wait until you can afford it. One way of looking at this; Say my household needs new transportation, I do not have enough money this year, so I am just going to send my local gov a bill for this regardless of their income etc. here is the bill and either pay up or get out! Of course, we as homeowners cannot do this, but essentially cities and towns can and do. This is wrong and in need of reform to "ability to pay" or "usage" taxing system! At least the 2% breaker, while not very effective, was an attempt to control an out of control system. An "income" circuit breaker that indicates your property tax bill can be no more that "X"% of your earned income would be more effective. Hopefully our legislature will fix this NOW!
12/12/2007

Anonymous said . . .

It never ceases to amaze me how school administrators view tax dollars as something they are entitled to receive. The 2% "circuit breaker" was designed to protect individual taxpayers—in other words, homeowners, your fellow citizens and YOU! Yet, Dr. Stock seems to think that pre-established budgets of his school system take precedent over that. "If you can't pay, then too darned bad! We have a budget to meet." Who cares, I suppose, about your personal budgets. If you've lived in your house for thirty years and worked your tail off to get it

paid off, well . . . too darned bad. Dr. Stock and his fellow adminis-
trators throughout the state don't care. Take the current market value
of your home, multiply it times 2% and just ask, "Is this enough?" Dr.
Stock says, NO! You should pay more. So, Dr. Stock, what would be a
fair cap? Care to say?
Some thinking just truly, truly amazes me.
2/12/2007

pyc said . . .

I guess I would have to agree with Anonymous number two. After
reading his/her thought free screed, I would guess that practically any
thinking would amaze him/her.
I don't particularly think I would be advertising that fact, however.
2/12/2007

stapleton said . . .

Anonymous Number 1, please provide a link that documents that
families in Indiana are losing their homes due to high property taxes.
While you are at it, please provide the links that show property taxes
have risen 25% over the last few years. Also, I would like to see a link
to the study showing that the reason Indiana is 6th in the nation in
home foreclosure rates is caused by, or even correlated to property
taxes.
One of the beauties of the internet is that when you make state-
ments, you can back up what you say with links that everyone else can
peruse. That way we can all increase our knowledge.
2/12/2007

Anonymous said . . .

Let's see, Dr. Stock . . .
You seem to speak out of both sides of your mouth on a regular ba-
sis. In this case, you have said that the 2% cap won't hurt Wawasee be-
cause it has such a low tax basis to begin with; however, it seems that

you regularly complain that Wawasee is unfairly compensated because it receives such a low percentage compared to the high tax rate. How can both of these arguments merit consideration?
2/12/2007

Anonymous said . . .

Stapleton:
The Indiana home foreclosure rate came from an Indy Star article dated 1/28/2007 Entitled "Indianapolis National Ranking Among Cities With Highest Foreclosure rate". The article simply indicated Indiana's rank in the nation. There is another Indy Star article entitled "Taxed Out" that spoke about Hoosiers Losing homes due to property taxes. Also WNDU 16 (4/21/2006) did an article entitled "Home Vacancies in South Bend Continue to Dissuade Investors". This article indicates the vacancy problem largely appears to be fallout from the property tax reassessment in 2003. You can also reference the Wed Sept 20th, 2006 Mail Journal to see a listing of tax sales in this area alone. Regarding the 15% avg income increase and 25% tax increase, first, I made a mistake the income increase is 14% and the avg property tax increase of 25% was correct. This can be found in the Sunday Sept 10th Indy Star and is entitled "Property Taxes set to Balloon". I can also share personal experience, my property taxes have increase 4 fold to the point they exceed my mortgage payments and if the 15% to 20% increase predicted this year alone occurs I will have to sell. Others I have spoken with have indicated 50%. Some are paying 25% of their income in property taxes! One local elderly lady had to sell a car to pay her taxes. Also, do you recall when the reassessment occurred? Local banks were advertising "property tax loans". If property taxes reflect "ability to pay" why were loans needed? Drastic reform is needed! What are we supposed to do just sign our paychecks over to our gov and schools? We are not talking about a $100 dollars any more, we are talking about $1,000's. We need to move away from assessed value to a system based on income (ability to pay) and usage (sales taxes)
2/12/2007

Anonymous said . . .

pyc must be one of Dr. Stock's fellow school administrators. How else could someone be so dismissive of clear and genuine concerns?
2/12/2007

also a taxpayer said . . .

What some of these articles fail to mention is the constant loss of manufacturing sector jobs in the state, and the increasing amount of layoffs. People who were working in these areas no longer have a stable income to rely on to manage their expenses. True, in the last reassessment for property taxes, a lot of homes did increase, but this is the price we pay for living in this area. I believe that the majority of the problems mentioned in the South Bend area dealt with landlords not being able to afford their rental properties because they are taxed in St. Joe county the same as owner occupied. Just my 2 cents. No one likes the idea of paying taxes, but they are inevitable. If they decrease property taxes, there will always be another tax to take its place-no matter what party is in control of the state or country.
2/12/2007

Dr. Mark J. Stock said . . .

Anonymous #3 said:
  In this case, you have said that the 2% cap won't hurt Wawasee because it has such a low tax basis to begin with; however, it seems that you regularly complain that Wawasee is unfairly compensated because it receives such a low percentage compared to the high tax rate.
  How can both of these arguments merit consideration?
  It sounds confusing because it is.
  Wawasee does not have a low tax "basis" (your words) it has a low tax "rate" (my words.) Tax "rate" is low when property values are high. This is because it doesn't take a very high rate to raise enough revenue to fund the state's school funding formula for the General Fund.

School districts that have low property values are compensated by the state with additional revenue to help keep their property taxes a little lower than they would have been.

The school funding formula was first put into place in the early 70's. Before that time local school boards controlled the GF tax rate. Schools that had low tax rates then were frozen and then the school funding formulas were instated. The new formula replaced local school board control of the GF with a state controlled formula. Since the 70's Wawasee has usually been lower than most school districts in funding per child, something that your local board does not control any longer.

My point about the 2% cap is that it is not likely to cause a Wawasee tax patron to exceed the 2% because there are enough high property values around that it drives the rate well below 2%. Our school rate is currently .89.

Even adding the local town's tax rates to ours is not likely to exceed 2% and if it did it would not be by much. A few financial institutions have run these numbers. The reports I heard did not show Wawasee having much of an impact. Other towns, cities and/or schools like South Bend could be in trouble.
2/13/2007

pyc said . . .

Thanks for the references, Anonymous. Some thoughts.

1. *The article, "Taxed Out" deals with the reassessment and specifically applies to property owners on the north side of Indianapolis. That area was hit hard because the old assessment rules ended up assessing those homes very low, when in reality the properties were worth hundreds of thousands of dollars (in some cases many hundreds of thousands.)*
2. *The article about Indianapolis ranking high among cities with foreclosures doesn't say anything at all about property taxes. Of course it doesn't say anything about predatory lending practices either, although some believe that is a contributing factor.*

3. *The article entitled "Property Taxes Set to Balloon" was interesting. Some things that were pointed out in the article include the fact that significant property tax hikes were seen in 2002 because many older homes had been largely undervalued (cf. number 1). Property taxes have risen in part because the inventory tax on business was eliminated. That's good for business, but bad for homeowners. When compared to other states, Indiana ranks 26th highest in the nation, or right about in the middle. Now, whether the fact that our property taxes rank us in the middle of the pack nationally constitutes a crisis is another question. I'll leave that to someone smarter than me.*
4. *The other articles I either couldn't find or don't really seem to relate. For instance a list of properties up for tax sale simply reflects that people didn't pay the tax on time. There could be various reasons why. The point is that simply because a property is listed doesn't indicate that high property taxes were the cause.*

I think most people are open to a discussion of a better way to fund government if there is one. Perhaps your suggestion of determining some way to tax based on ability to pay is the way to go. But if so, shouldn't someone have thought up a plan to make that happen before they started taking funds away? (I could make a snarky remark about Republicans and plans, but that is off topic) Anyway, it's an interesting discussion.
2/13/2007

Anonymous said . . .

PYC—yes this is a very interesting discussion. I do not think the ranking has much to do with our problems. I believe Indiana is also in the upper half regarding "total tax burden". (do not happen to have that reference) Most of the current issues were caused by very poor planning during the switch over to a market value system. Folks that purchased homes 40 years ago, at a price they could afford at the time, now to be told their property is worth hundreds of thousands and by the way your tax bill is going from $1,500 per year to $6,000 per year

is unfair. I do not believe any family should be taxed out of their primary residence hence my wish to move towards a better metric of ability to pay such as income taxes. The current system was established when owning land really meant wealth as one could produce more corn, cattle etc. They actually made money from their land. For most of us this is no longer true until we sell and not always then either. This is an outdated system. As a matter of fact the Indiana Fiscal Policy Institute released a study on Oct 20, 2005 that indicates among other things that "The type, quantity, and quality of data currently collected will not support a market value assessment system". So now we are trying to use an old system, based on a meaningless metric that is not sufficient to create a fair tax. Again, poor planning. The entire "pay up or get out" mentality harkens back to feudal times! With the above in mind, just as we do at home, our gov needs to cut spending!!!!
2/13/2007

pyc said . . .

Anonymous, you raise some good issues. And again, whether taxing property is the best way to fund governmental services is something that I will leave to people smarter than myself. My guess, however, is that if it were simple, a new system would already be in place. Rather, it seems to me that because the situation is rather complex, whatever solution is reached will need to address all of those complexities. And unfortunately, in many places, the realities of the loss of funding as a result of 2% cap, is much closer than that solution.
2/13/2007

Anonymous said . . .

Thanks to all who left comments on this subject. I do not feel like I know the subject well enough to enter in on the debate but I love reading how others feel about it. This is why I like Dr. Stock's blog so much. I feel like I learn more here than I do from reading the newspaper.

Again, thanks to everyone for this learning experience! Keep the top-
ics coming Doc Stock!!
An avid reader
2/14/2007

This is a clear example of using the blog site as an educational tool for informing your community. It is especially helpful on complex matters that can be explained in small doses
over several days or weeks. The interaction with the public on
complex issues such as this can create a sense of trust and respect for the school leader and the difficulties they encounter
on a daily basis.

On some occasions I would run a post called "Wednesday Wonderings," in which I would run frequently asked questions that I
often heard from school patrons.

Here is one example of such a post.

Wednesday Wonderings
  Did you ever wonder why?

  1. *Did you ever wonder why so many WCSC buses run around half*
     empty half the time?
       This might come as a surprise to the mathematically chal-
     lenged :-) . . . but 100% of Wawasee's buses run at 50% capacity
     half the time. We had a plan to create 100% efficiency 100% of
     the time but the parents didn't want to drive their kids to the bus
     driver's house!
  2. *Did you ever wonder why Wawasee has the second highest prop-*
     erty values per student in the state but has always ranked in the
     bottom quarter in revenue per student?
       Due to high property wealth here, a low tax rate generates a
     lot of money so the state withholds state revenue and sends it to
     schools with higher "needs." While our "needy" students are in-
     creasing, they must not be increasing as fast as other school
     districts.

3. *Did you ever wonder why property taxes are unpopular but school superintendents are reluctant to support getting rid of it in favor of other taxes?*

    The property tax is a stable, if unpopular tax. Students are always with us and always need education no matter what the economy is doing. If we switch to sales taxes and income taxes to fund schools, then revenue streams are erratic and float up and down with the economy. While a business can lay off employees during a downtime, schools always have students whether their parents have jobs or not. It's hard to "layoff" students to make ends meet and outsourcing students to third world countries doesn't appear popular either!

4. *Did you ever wonder why the school can afford athletic programs but it scrimps and saves in other areas?*

    Athletic programs are entirely self-supporting except for the coaches' stipends and some large facility expenditures. Cutting athletics will not help the instructional program in any way.

5. *Did you ever wonder why a school district can build a new building but it can't increase personnel to staff it?*

    Facilities are paid for from a different fund and the school cannot transfer building project money over to the General Fund where personnel costs come from. SO . . . it is true, your school system could conceivably build a "Taj Mahal" but not raise taxes to hire more teachers. The school boards have a lot of control over Debt Service Funds to pay for buildings but almost no control over the General Fund to pay for staffing.

    Have you ever "wondered" about a school issue? E-mail it to me (link is on the sidebar) and I will make a list and try to answer some frequently asked questions about schools.

    Have a great Thanksgiving Break!!!!!

Posted by Superintendent, Dr. Mark J. Stock at 12:13 PM

These lengthy posts and subsequent comments from the public help to illustrate the potential use for blogs to educate community members on various questions that come up from time to time, often with a little sense of humor thrown in. I would often keep track of various questions I was asked because I assumed if one person had a question, others would too.

This post along with the lengthy comments provided give a good example of the type of edgy interaction that accompanies online discourse.

Does blogging take thick skin? Of course it does. But being an educational leader in today's world means living under a microscope and one advantage to blogging is that it puts the leader in a more proactive mode of dealing with the public.

However, like most things in life, there are some disadvantages and barriers that have to be overcome. Chapter three will review some of the barriers and problems with blogging.

3

BARRIERS AND PROBLEMS WITH BLOGGING

"Rinnnggggg."

The harsh sound of the phone ringing broke the peaceful silence.

I folded up the evening newspaper and reached down for the lever on the side of the recliner. Lifting myself out of the chair I tried to catch the phone before the harsh ring interrupted the silence again.

"Hello?" I asked.

"Hi, this is Diane from central office. I am sorry to interrupt your evening at home but I thought you might want to know what is on the blog site tonight under comments," said the voice on the line.

"No worries. I was just reading the paper," I said. "What kind of comments?" I added.

"Well, someone has put up some very rude comments about the building principal and I thought they were inappropriate and I knew you wouldn't approve of them," she said. "I know your blog policy is not to allow people to openly criticize individual employees."

"Except for me," I chuckled. I continued, "The superintendent is always fair game, but you are right. I don't allow comments that single out individuals. Criticizing district or school policies or procedures is fair enough, but we do ask patrons to talk to individuals personally about individual complaints."

"Well, you'll want to read these. The comments do not pertain to your blog post today. Not only are they off topic but they are very rude and bordering on vulgar," she added.

"Thanks for the heads up, Diane. I'll get right on it. See you in the morning."

I hung up the phone and headed for the computer. After clicking on "The Wawascene" site, I scrolled down to the comments section and located the offending comment.

I went into administrative mode and deleted the offending comment. In its place I reminded patrons about the blog policy of keeping comments on topic and avoiding criticism of individual employees.

I took the added safety of freezing all existing comments and shutting off all new comments for the evening so that I wouldn't have to monitor the site all evening.

I headed back to evening paper and the recliner chair, thinking about the handful of disadvantages that go along with being a blogging school administrator.

In the previous chapter I spent some time extolling the virtues of being a school leader who blogs and providing examples of blog posts that help promote the educational leader's agenda. But what about the disadvantages? There are some drawbacks to blogging that must be acknowledged.

Perhaps the most obvious drawback to blogging is that written words are often open to misinterpretation.

WRITTEN WORDS CAN BE MISUNDERSTOOD

It is a common understanding that much of successful communication is based on nonverbal communication. The gestures and facial expressions of individuals provide much context and background for the words we speak. In an online environment, the absence of these nonverbal clues is often problematic. Complicating the issue further is the anonymous nature of many online interactions. In face-to-face interactions it is common to know some of the background and perceived motivations of the individuals you are interacting with. In the rough-and-tumble world of online communication this is seldom the case.

The written words are often misinterpreted and seldom softened by the subtleties and niceties of personal contact. These difficulties are then compounded by the complexities of typing and navigating the technical aspects of the online medium. Because keyboarding can be awkward and even tedious for many people, they get straight to the point. And that point is often blunt and even rude at times. When people do not take the time for the personal kindnesses that accompany personal interactions, the cold hard facts and opinions dished out in online chat rooms and discussion boards can provoke the worst in people. Most people that frequent online boards develop thick skin pretty quickly—or they leave and do not come back.

Like most technological inventions, the social changes usually drag along behind the technology. It will be interesting to see if people become more socially aware and sensitive in online environments or whether we just adapt and accept the perceived bluntness of current online interaction.

Another drawback to blogging for the educational leader is the fact that once the issues are put out on the blog site, you can't run from them any longer.

YOU CAN'T RUN FROM THE CONTROVERSY

When a patron raises a controversial issue to a school leader in private, the ripples are small and often the leader has some time to determine a course of action to respond to the patron's concerns. In the "instant gratification" world of Internet interactions, the controversial issue is instantly placed in front of hundreds or even thousands of readers, often before the moderator or administrator of the blog has even seen the question or comment.

Then, the leader's response to that question or issue is immediately apparent to all who lurk in the background as readers. The speed of these interactions is far greater and farther reaching than traditional forums such as letters written to the editors of the local papers. In many cases the speed of these interactions can play to the leader's advantage, but in many cases it can be problematic. Because it is so easy for a patron to pass along the information or the link provided on the blog site, news can travel at the speed of light on the Internet.

YOUR WORDS MAY SEEM TO LAST FOREVER

As a blogger, the content you put up on the blog site will stay in the archives unless you go in and delete sections of the blog. When you have your own blog, of course you always have the option of deleting the entire blog. But as a school leader you may end up creating a blogging "institution" that the local community values as an information source. When you leave the school or school district does the blog end? Can you take it with you? Will the new person choose to utilize the source? What do you do with all the existing content since it is yours? What if your opinion changes over time and there are posts still in the archives that reflect another view? It is important to remember that when you blog you are speaking to the entire world and even though you may choose to delete sections of your blog that doesn't mean that readers have not saved your material.

Perhaps one of the biggest drawbacks to blogging is that it takes time out of an educational leader's busy day.

IT TAKES TIME

Blogging takes time. There is no way around it. This may be the most frequent question I get from school leaders who are thinking about blogging. The busy school leader finds it hard to imagine where they are going to find time to blog during their frenetically paced work life. While it does take time, this concern is not as problematic as most think. A blogging superintendent or school principal under normal circumstances can plan on spending anywhere from ten minutes a day up to an hour a day blogging.

The time spent can vary widely based the leader's comfort level with blogging technology and the type of blogging they choose to do. Most of the blogging software—such as Blogger, Typepad, LiveJournal, and others—has become so user friendly that most new bloggers can be up and blogging live in twenty minutes or so. Of course what inevitably happens is that the blogger gets interested in the more advanced features and then spends extra time playing with audio blogging, video clips, and making the blog site more attractive by adding third party features such as stat counters, weather stickers, and other miscellaneous extras. But this is part of the fun and most bloggers do not consider this as part of the time commitment for actual blogging content. In districts where the leaders have access to technology experts, this is farmed out and the leader almost exclusively concentrates on the content for the blog site.

Most blogging leaders develop some type of routine so that blogging becomes integrated into daily work life. Here is a typical day when I was a blogging school superintendent.

TYPICAL DAY IN THE LIFE OF A BLOGGING SUPERINTENDENT

This is a composite view of numerous experiences I have had with blogging. All of these are real although they are combined from several different experiences.

7:23 AM

I tossed my coat on the table, turned on the computer, and sat down at the desk with a cup of steaming black coffee. I took a careful sip and while the computer loaded, I walked over to the in-basket and looked for any notes or handouts from Director of Finance Jim Evans, Curriculum Director Joy Goshert, or Special Education Director Wendy Hite. These talented individuals, who were part of our management team, often placed articles or web links in my in-basket as potential blog fodder. Sure enough, sitting on top of the stack was a copy of an article Jim had printed off about an alternative view of America's alleged obesity crisis. The article was taking pot shots at legislation that was trying to require schools to report the body mass index (BMI) of every student and then report this data to the state department. Indiana legislators were currently considering just such a bill.

I read the article and noted that there were several good points made and several assumptions that just seemed wrong-headed to me. I noted the URL and then turned to the computer and found the online version of a related article. I then started a blog post describing a position on the issue and hyperlinked to the online legislation so that patrons could see the actual bill that required schools to track and report the BMI of every student. I reminded them that they could use the Legislative Sticker on the sidebar of the website to contact their legislator by e-mail if they had an opinion about this bill.

7:35 AM

I finished up the blog post, ran spell checker, and read it one more time. Satisfied, I clicked "post" and sent the message off into cyberspace. I then clicked "view blog" so I could see what the patrons would see when they accessed the blog site. I grimaced when I noticed an awkward sentence. I immediately went into edit mode, corrected the awkward sentence, and then republished the post. I went back to the "view blog" button, clicked it, and read the new version. Liking it much better, I let it stand.

7:42 AM

I slurped the now lukewarm coffee, turned to the stack of mail in the inbox, and waded into the stack.

8:25 AM

Looking up from my mail, I looked out the window and wondered if the public had any reaction to my postings. I refreshed the screen on the blog site and noticed that there were two patron comments. Scrolling down the post I noticed the first comment took a slap at the school lunches in their child's school and the second comment noted that the legislation should be enacted. Noticing that neither poster had asked any direct questions or indicated they needed a response from me, I decided not to respond.

1:35 PM

After a round of meetings and conferences, I returned to the office and briefly checked on the site again between phone calls. Nothing new, although the stat counter program showed there were several thousand more hits on the site.

2:00 PM

I spent the remainder of the day returning phone calls, answering e-mails, and talking to several principals.

8:37 PM

While surfing the net at home, I checked the blog site one more time. Seeing nothing unusual, I checked the weather report for the next day and headed for the easy chair and the evening newspaper to unwind.

This account pretty well sums up a normal day in the experience of a blogging school superintendent. While it is difficult for any school administrator to try and describe a "typical" day, this is a fair representation of how much time it takes when things are somewhat normal. I believe that the time spent blogging was in most cases a wise investment. In addition to the ever-present concern over time, another potential disadvantage for the blogging school leader is the use of the technology itself.

TROUBLE FOR THE TECHNOPHOBE

Despite the user-friendly style of most popular blogging software, the truly technophobic leader may still find it a little awkward at first. I have found most of the free blog sites have gone to point-

and-click versions that generally require nothing more than making menu selections to get started. In the early days of blogging, a person needed some knowledge of HTML to make changes to the websites. Current software requires very little technology background other than a basic familiarity with computers and a little awareness of how online interaction works.

Since many teachers and students are now blogging, it is not unusual for the blogging school leader to turn to others for a little support when they get stuck. For most new bloggers, the tough part is not getting started, it usually occurs when they get comfortable enough to want to start customizing the website to make it more personal. This is when it is easy to fritter away two hours playing with some third-party function such as adding a new statistics counter to keep tabs on your site traffic.

In addition to the time commitment, another drawback to blogging is the frustration problem of handling anonymous comments on the blog.

DEALING WITH THE ANONYMITY OF BLOG COMMENTS

The potential for an anonymous lurker to spew negativity on a blog site is perhaps the most fearful aspect of blogging for most school administrators. While superintendents and other school leaders tend to grow somewhat calloused to detractors, the idea of intentionally opening up and allowing such a free environment to exist runs counterintuitive to many leaders. School leaders have traditionally played turtle to such negativity, quietly pulling into their shell and hoping the negativity goes away. It's a new age folks. It's not going away.

If you don't have a current established and controlled forum for dealing with the negativity openly, then the negative person will open up their own site and spew the negativity unrestrained and uninhibited. By having an established blog site with established readers, the blogging leader can set a positive and interactive stage that will flush out the negative individuals and in most cases expose them to the wider public. The negative poster often thinks that many people think like they do. When a negative poster puts up a comment that takes a slap at someone or something going on in the school system, in many instances they are immediately pounced on by other individuals with a contrary view. This give and take is often what continues to bring people to the blog site. While the blog moderator posts the initial content, it is often the give and take of the opinions of the readers that brings people back to the site over and over.

Leaders who are considering blogging should consider starting their blog with the comment features turned off, especially if the fear of negative comments is a concern for them. It is much easier to turn the comments on later and open up the forum than to start out with comments on and then turn them off when controversy strikes. The politically savvy school leader will recognize that community patrons will view it as censorship or, even worse, think their leader is too thin skinned to handle a little controversy on the discussion board.

Well, I have taken some time to discuss the pros and cons of blogging, but how do you know if blogging is for you?

HOW TO KNOW IF BLOGGING IS FOR YOU

There are a number of questions that you might consider asking yourself prior to making a decision to start a blog. Darren Rowse (2008) proposes the following twenty-three questions that you might think about prior to beginning your blog. The questions in italics are Darren's but I have added content to the explanations.

1. *Do you enjoy writing?* If you don't enjoy writing, then this medium is not for you. On the other hand, if you have never tried to write a little something every day about topics of interest to you, then maybe you should try it! If you don't type (there may still be a few of those left!) then you will need someone to post your scribbling for you just from the sheer time commitment it would take to hunt and peck your way to blog stardom.

2. *What's your message?* Do you have a specific purpose in mind or do you just want to start right in? Is there a specific need in your school district that you want to address? Is blogging the right forum for it?

3. *Are you a good communicator?* You don't have to be a world class writer or communicator to start a blog. Often the best blogs simply come from the heart and reflect items and issues of importance to you. However, if simple grammar, spelling, and punctuation are a chore for you, then you will need to develop some help along these lines before blogging. Online environments tend to be somewhat forgiving on these type of issues, but as the superintendent of schools or the principal of the school you will not be given the same leeway as other members of the community. The community will expect more of you. You will need to be able to provide simple language, written in simple style. but it must be grammatically correct with good spelling and punctuation.

4. *Are you better at writing or speaking?* Most educators are gifted verbally because they tend to make a living with their voice more than their pen. In this case, you might consider putting some podcasts up on your site or posting video clips to take advantage of this skill.

5. *Do you want to be the central voice on your website?* Blogs don't have to be one voice. Some very good blogs are group blogs where everyone takes a turn as blogger in order to spread the

work around. This is a great strategy in a school district where there might be several central office employees available to help blog. In the scenario of group blogging, everyone may be responsible for posting once a week and reading every day. By having multiple eyes monitoring the site you are able to spread the burden around so one person doesn't feel the daily pressure to manage the site. Just remember that the leader's presence speaks to the importance of it and if the leader isn't a prominent voice on the blog then it might not be as popular unless the other group bloggers are talented, funny, and interesting in their own right.

6. *Are you a self-starter?* Starting up a blog site does take a little initiative although it is quite simple. The difficult part comes down the line after you think you have exhausted most of what you had to say in the beginning. This is the point when you realize that you don't have to be creating new content all the time. You simply need to hyperlink to other articles and news items on your blog. This does mean however, that you must be an active reader of online news and blogs so that you have content to link to.

7. *Are you disciplined?* Can you motivate yourself to post or link to posts every day? How about multiple times a week? Patrons will forgive you for a few missed posts, but if they come back three or four times and see nothing new, don't look for them to return.

8. *Do you have time? Will you make time?* Remember it isn't just posting something new every day that takes time. You also have to read their comments, respond to their comments, read other bloggers, and link to other bloggers.

9. *Are you thick skinned?* This is a big one. You must develop thicker skin to blog successfully. When people agree with you, blogging is easy, but you may be surprised at the variety of opinions on various topics. Bloggers with thin skin

do not last very long. It is just too uncomfortable. But remember this little tidbit. When someone posts a negative comment that comes out of left field and is clearly off the wall, someone with common sense will almost always rise to take exception to it. This happened so often to me as a blogger that I came to the conclusion that blogging was a success just because it exposed the crazies to people with common sense.

10. *Are you willing to be in the public spotlight?* I assume because you have some interest in educational administration that you may have already gotten over this hurdle. Just remember that blogging will increase your public profile and while most of it will be positive, there will always be a negative element associated with blogging.

11. *Do you have any technical ability? Do you have access to tech support in your school district?* You don't have to be tech savvy to do this, but it helps. You can blog successfully as a newbie as long as you have someone internally to call on if you get stuck.

12. *Do you take yourself too seriously?* Have a sense of humor! Nothing helps your blog like a little humor. In addition to "Friday's Funnies," where I posted funny stories about kids, I occasionally posted a satire piece. However, I made sure that I labeled it satire because you would be surprised how many people can take you even more seriously than you take yourself!

13. *Do you have a blend of humility and ego?* Nothing comes across as authentic as a big helping of humble pie. As a blogger, I used to admit my mistakes and this usually generated an element of kindness from others. When I made a bad decision on cancelling school in inclement weather, I would admit that on the blog. Several people with common sense would acknowledge that they understood how

difficult it was to predict the weather. Someone else would chime in and blast me anyway. I found that blogging in general elicited a certain amount of public goodwill simply because they admired my courage to be "out there."

14. *Are you willing to learn?* Blogging is a journey and it will take time to build your leadership and your comfort levels. You will grow with the technology and learn as you go. Will you stick with it long enough to learn the basics and get comfortable with it?

15. *Do you enjoy reading?* The essence of being a good blogger is to be a good reader. If you don't scour the daily educational news for potential blogging topics, you will be out of material in three weeks. Once you have exhausted what's in your head (only took a few days for me!) you will need more material. I put several major newspapers and several educational news services on my favorites list and checked them every morning. This gives you a quick sense of what's going on in education around the world.

16. *Are you an organized person?* This isn't totally necessary, but it helps tremendously. As a superintendent, I found that blogging was what I did in between other things. Your day is often dictated by others, but you must squeeze the time in to monitor the blog and post regularly.

17. *Are you a social person?* The most successful bloggers find some way to be authentic in their postings. People connect with them. They interact through responding to comments and posting thoughts and opinions that strike the readers as genuine. Are you approachable?

18. *Do you enjoy virtual relationships?* Some social people are terrible in online interactions. They are much better face-to-face than they are in online forums. The good news is

that online interaction can be learned, but it takes some time and practice for some people.

19. *Are you a creative person?* This isn't a necessity but it helps. As a superintendent or principal you may have some form of "captive" audience that other bloggers might not have. So even if your site isn't captivating and visually appealing, you may still have some readers. However, giving a sense of creativity and originality to your blog site will enhance your readership beyond the people just in your school or school district.

20. *Do you have stick-ability?* Some blogs may be overnight successes but most of them take time to develop a community of readers.

21. *Are you consistent? Do you change your blogging style midstream?* No one wants to read a boring blog but it may be more important to be consistent in your style and voice than to change constantly and leave people wondering what the point is to your blog.

22. *Are you honest and transparent?* This one is huge. As an educational leader people will want to get some sense of who you are. Who is this person responsible for my children every day? What do they believe? What are their philosophies? The online forum can be one way for to help people who don't interact with you in real time to still get to know you.

23. *Are you willing to work hard?* Virtually all educational leaders are willing to work hard. But are you willing to work hard at blogging?

While most educational leaders do not intend to make blogging a separate occupation, the questions are still useful in helping us take a well-rounded look at all the implications of blogging on a regular basis.

We have examined the roots of blogging; the advantages and disadvantages of blogging; and the types of things a potential blogger should consider before diving into the blogosphere.

Now I will show you how to start and grow your own blog in chapter four.

4

HOW TO START
AND GROW YOUR
OWN BLOG

So you want to be a blogger now? I haven't scared you off yet? Getting started is quite simple but there are some things that you need to consider before starting the actual process of blogging.

If you are an educational leader or involved as an employee in education at some level, you should consider telling your boss about what you intend to do.

STEP ONE: INFORM YOUR SUPERIORS

Inform your immediate supervisors, whether that is your school board or your superintendent, about your intentions and why you want to blog. Be sure you have read numerous blogs and noted the style and format of blogging. Make sure you are clear as to whether your superiors understand your purpose for blogging and who you are attempting to represent when you blog. Is this a personal blog? Are you representing yourself, the school, or the school district?

The higher the leadership position the more difficult it is to separate your personal views from the views of the organization. After presenting my initial blog site to the school board in a public school board meeting, our board asked me to put a disclaimer on the site indicating that I was representing my own personal views and did not claim to represent the school board or any individual school board member's views.

Here is the disclaimer statement I posted on the blog.

While this site operates with the knowledge and awareness of the Wawasee Community School Board, the content and opinions posted here may or may not represent their views personally or collectively, nor does it attempt to represent the official viewpoint of Wawasee administrators or employees.

Placing a disclaimer on your site is helpful in that it provides your superiors a little plausible deniability so that you aren't putting them out on a limb on a particular topic or view that they might not have in common with you.

After you have informed your bosses that you wish to start blogging, spend some time to find the best software for your blog.

STEP TWO: CHOOSE YOUR BLOGGING SOFTWARE

There are many different blog sites that offer free or inexpensive blogging software and free hosting for your blog content. Start by checking out Blogger, LiveJournal, TypePad, or others and check out the features, and any potential costs.

Here is a short list of potential blog platforms you might consider.

1. Blogger.com: This is the most popular and perhaps one of the most user-friendly blog platforms available. It is a free service and you can host your content on their servers or your own.
2. Easyjournal: This blog platform is free.
3. Tribe.net: This blog platform is free.
4. Radio Userland: This is software that you purchase and it requires server space for publishing.
5. TypePad: There is a cost to use this blog platform but it is a popular one.
6. Xanga: This blog platform is free.
7. WordPress: This blog platform is free.

There are many other blog platforms that are available and easy to locate through a simple Internet search. Many of them are free as a basic service and then provide additional upgrades and options for additional fees. Some may require advertising on your site and some will allow advertising as an option. If you think blogging may be a long-term project for you then you should take time to find a site that you really like. Moving your content from one blog platform to another can be a tricky endeavor. Remember, you may have developed a loyal following and when you move platforms you not only have technical issues in moving all your content from one server to another, but you are also changing your URL. This is like changing your postal address and your physical location. People may have trouble finding you again.

There are other things you should consider when you think about choosing a blogging platform. When I started blogging as a superintendent I did not want any public monies to go toward this endeavor because I wanted this site to be a personal blog site. I choose Blogger because they provided the platform, the domain name, and the hosting for free. They also allow you to put the blog up without ads. Since I was just experimenting in the beginning I did not want to invest any money and I wanted the simplest startup possible. I never got the chance to switch over to another platform because the site got so popular quickly that I didn't feel that I could switch to something else and confuse people.

In most cases, the blog sites will allow you to set up a blog and try it out. In most cases you can delete the entire blog at any time. You can also set the blog up so that only the people you identify can access the blog. This is an excellent way to get started if you want to experiment without your blog being visible to everyone on the Internet.

Once you have chosen a blog platform and software it is time to set up your blog site.

STEP THREE: SET UP YOUR BLOG SITE

There are many choices to make when setting up your blog. Most of these choices are menu-driven and do not require any technical background to get started. To help the neophyte, there are usually default choices that present the most standard and popular settings when you come to a setting that you do not understand. The range of decisions go from the basic colors and font styles of how your blog will look, to the way your blog will archive all your posts. Almost all the choices you make can be changed later when you get more comfortable with how the blog software works. The average person who is somewhat familiar with computers can be up and blogging in twenty minutes.

When you set up your blog site you will need to determine whether to go with a hosted platform or a standalone platform.

Hosted Platform

A hosted platform is what most beginning bloggers start out with because they are often free. Blogger.com is an example of a free, hosted blog platform. Blogger.com will provide you with a web address, also referred to as the URL. This URL is often a combination of their URL and your own blog name. For example, when I was blogging as superintendent of the Wawasee Community School Corporation, I used the URL of www.wawasee.blogspot .com. You can see the name of the school district and the URL of blogspot.com, which was the URL for the Blogger.com platform.

These blog platforms are "hosted" because they host your blog site on their own domain name and provide server space for your content. All you need is a connection to the Internet.

There are pros and cons to using hosted platforms.

Pros

1. Free (or inexpensive): Most hosted options are free.
2. Easy to get started: Most of the free sites can be set up with default templates in a very short time. The blogger usually makes a few menu-driven selections. If the blogger is relatively new to the technology this is the way to go.
3. Easy to run: Once the blogger has set up the blog and made the menu selections the blog is very easy to maintain. Posting to the blog usually means typing in the boxes and hitting "publish." In newer versions of Microsoft Word you can even publish to your blog right from your software without going to your blog site first.
4. Search engine benefits: In most of the hosted platforms, your blog will get ranked pretty quickly if you get some site

traffic. It is easier to get ranked on the search engines quickly when you use a hosted platform.

Cons

1. Not as customizable: If you have a keen interest in blogging you will soon find that you wish you could customize your blog template. With hosted platforms, your options are more limited. While things have improved dramatically in recent years, there is still less flexibility on hosted platforms. Like most things, the more user-friendly it is, the fewer customizing options are available. In fact, most hosted platforms end up looking very similar.
2. Less control: If you run your blog on a hosted platform, you have less control over the technology problems. If the site is down, you have no choice but to wait it out. On very rare occasions the Blogger.com site was down and I would be frustrated as a blogger. It normally was not a problem except on a few days when there were time-sensitive postings, such as information regarding a school closure or cancellation.
3. Upgrading to standalone hosting can be tough: If you chose to move your blog content from a hosted platform to a standalone platform, you could run into difficulties. Your readers may have gotten used to your domain name and now you have created another one. You will also start at the bottom of the search engine ratings all over again as you switch to the new domain name.

The menu driven choices found on hosted blog platforms will have their own style and method of site development. Just know that the choices are fairly clear and mostly nontechnical so that the newbie can simply choose default choices and be up and running fairly quickly.

Once you have decided what blog platform to use, you will need to decide how much public interaction you want.

STEP FOUR: DECIDE HOW MUCH PUBLIC INTERACTION YOU WANT

These are the most important decisions that a school leader will make when deciding to blog. There are a range of options available when deciding what type of public interaction you will allow on your blog. These options range from no public comments at all and limited public visibility, to unlimited anonymous public comments and unlimited public visibility on the web. These options range from a very restrictive and limited public presence to a wide open public forum.

I will review your choices with the most restrictive choices first. Most blog experts will recommend that the publicly visible leader start by limiting public input and interaction in the beginning until the blogger is comfortable with the forum.

The most restrictive format is to start quietly by only allowing selected members to view your blog and limiting their ability to make comments.

No Public Interaction and Limited Public Visibility on the Web

The blogger can decide to leave the comment functions turned off and only allow selected individuals the ability to view the blog. This means that not only is the communication on the blog site one-way communication, but also only a few individuals will be given the ability to access the blog site. The blogger who is just getting started might consider only providing access to a few invited people and even leaving the comments turned off.

This option might work for the new blogger who is not only nervous about the public visibility, but also might be nervous about how blogging works and whether they will have the discipline to keep the blog current. There isn't much use for this type of blogging for the leader except for the experimental benefits. However, if the blogging experiment fails, only a few people will know you even tried! This makes it a low- to no-risk effort.

The next least restrictive option would be to allow some public interaction with limited public visibility on the web.

Limited Public Interaction with Limited Public Visibility on the Web

In this scenario, the blogger leaves the public comments open, but only allows selected members to be able to access the blog. An example might be a superintendent who wants to experiment with the blog site but only provides access to administrators while working out the bugs. In this case the blog site would be password protected and only individuals who were invited would be able to see the blog site. They would, however, be able to use the comment function to leave comments for the other invited members to see.

Outside of the educational setting, a typical use for this type of blog might be a family scattered across the world that wants to keep up with each other but doesn't want the rest of the world looking at their pictures and commentary. Many family blogs are set up this way. This option is a viable choice for the blogging leader who is experimenting but doesn't want to make the blog openly visible, yet would like to see how the comment functions work. These choices are made by menu-driven selections in the settings tabs of most blog platform software.

Moving up the least restrictive continuum we might open up the public visibility of the blog site to the open public but leave the comment feature turned off.

No Public Interaction but Open Public Visibility on the Web

In this scenario, the blogger chooses to leave the public comment functions turned off but leaves the blog open to any person in the world who stumbles across this site. This is the most common and perhaps the best way to get started for a school leader who is semi-comfortable with blogging software and the use of the blog site, but wishes to ease into the rough-and-tumble world of Internet interactions. It is easier to turn on the public comment function later on a specific post. The blogging leader who intends to use the blog site similar to an online newsletter might choose this option. This would be the most common way that an educational leader might choose to get started.

Continuing up the least restrictive continuum, we might next consider providing an open presence to the public of the blog site but only allow public comments with the approval of the blogger.

Open Public Interaction with Blog Moderator Approval and Open Visibility on the Web

In this scenario, the blog moderator allows patrons to leave comments but only after the comment is mailed to the blog moderator, who must approve the comment before the blog site allows it to be posted. This is a good option for getting started but it does require the blog moderator to monitor their e-mails frequently. As a blogging superintendent, I started out this way but quickly grew tired of approving every comment. After a while I simply changed the settings for comment approval and allowed all comments to be posted. The blog moderator will still have to monitor the blog closely because there will be situations where some comments will have to be deleted. Some hosted platforms give the moderator the choice of deleting the entire comment, or deleting the comment and leaving a placeholder that lets the public know that the moderator has removed a comment. In this option the blog site is openly visible on the Internet but the comments posted by the public require prior approval.

The next least restrictive option would be to allow open public visibility but to allow comments only from people who have registered and provided an e-mail address.

Open Public Interaction for Registered Users Only and Open Public Visibility

In this scenario, the commenter can still be anonymous if they wish but they have to register and provide an e-mail address. Of course they can still use an e-mail address that does not identify them, but it does discourage the "drive-by" negative commenter because they have to go to the trouble of registering first. The blog site would still be visible to anyone. This has become a fairly popular option because it does tend to limit mean and lazy people. Mean people can still register and leave you a scathing comment, though, but they must make the extra effort to register.

The least restrictive of all choices is to allow open public visibility of your blog and to allow unlimited anonymous public comments.

Open Public Interaction and Open Public Visibility

This might be the most common blogging format. In this scenario the blogger would leave the comments function on and would allow open public access to the site. Any person who stumbled onto this URL would not only be able to see the blog site but could also leave an anonymous comment. This type of blog promotes the highest readership and creates the most community input. It also provides an open forum for every person and hence must be monitored regularly.

From a negative perspective it also allows unlimited anonymous comments and thus puts a lot of pressure on the blog moderator to monitor the site so that inappropriate comments can be deleted.

OTHER DECISIONS TO MAKE AFTER SETTING UP YOUR BLOG SITE

Statistics: You might consider adding a statistics counter to keep track of your Internet traffic. There are a variety of third-party statistics counters that you can add to your blog in order to monitor and track your visitors. One of the great features most of them provide is information regarding the referring links to your site. This information will tell you what websites and blog sites your visitors are viewing on their way to view your blog. You will find it quite fascinating when you click on your statistics page and see a colorful map of the world pop up with a colored pin showing every corner of the globe your visitors are coming from.

Advertisements: You might also consider adding advertisements to generate revenue for your organization if you find the site traffic is high enough. You could use one of the commercial ad programs or you can consider putting local ads from businesses and organizations within your community.

Polling software: You may have noticed on many blog sites a little polling sticker in the corner that asks your opinion on something. If you click on the sticker, a window will pop up that shows you how many people have voted and what their choices were.

The purpose is primarily to drive up traffic because every time you click on the site the statistic counter will go up again. This hit counter is what drives up advertising rates.

A blogging superintendent could find an occasional use for a mini-poll for school district purposes. Below you will see a post from "The Wawascene" that refers to a mini-poll that I placed on the top of the blog site asking patrons about what television and radio stations they preferred to listen to for school closing announcements.

> *Mark's Mini-Poll*
> *Trying hard to be a good public servant and not a lazy slacker . . .*
> *:-) . . . I have created a mini-poll of several popular radio stations that we can add to the call list if there is a demand for it. We can also poll on TV stations next week.*
> *I will leave the poll up for about a week.*
> *(Note: I have set it up so you can only vote once in case you were wondering why you couldn't vote 1,000 times :-)*
> *Now . . . No whining if yours isn't picked!!! :-)*
> *Posted by Superintendent, Dr. Mark J. Stock at 8:19 PM*

The funny little reference in the post about "being a good public servant and not a lazy slacker" was a referral to person who made a tongue-in-cheek comment on an earlier post about me being a "slacker" if I didn't call every media outlet within forty-five miles of the school district. The person making the post was defending me with a little veiled sarcasm of the critics who were posting.

Other options include adding weather stickers, links to other educational organizations, or other third-party add-ons that can make your blog site more attractive and more interesting to your readers.

GROWING YOUR BLOG

No matter how much effort you have spent designing a world class blog template and developing quality content for the site; your blog is only useful to others when they actually read it. Expanding your readership and increasing the traffic to your blog site is the next step.

Here are a few simple strategies I used to increase blog readership in a small community while I was superintendent of schools. The statistics counter I used showed the average during peak time ranged from two thousand hits to seven thousand hits per day on the blog site. The highest was seventy-one thousand hits in one day from approximately twenty-one thousand visitors. For newbies it might be important to point out that most statistics packages allow you to choose several different options for how the statistics are counted. A "visitor" was defined on this blog as a computer that accessed the site during a thirty minute period. If the person logged out and returned later, they would be counted as another visitor. However, if they clicked on various parts of the site twenty times during that thirty minute period, it would register as twenty separate hits on the site but still just one visitor.

For the serious blogger, these site statistics become the critical feedback that tells you how you are doing. You will be able to monitor the peak usage and the location of your visitors and what sites they came from on their way to your blog. This feedback will help you as you begin to find what works and what doesn't.

There are several simple strategies that I used to kick start my blog. I started by informing all the employees in the school district that I was starting a blog.

E-mail the Link to Your Employees

Start by e-mailing your link to all your employees and ask them to bookmark the site or consider making it their home page on their school computers. The key to expanding your readership starts with getting your employees to check the site regularly. You can also ask them to forward the link to others they know in their community and even to the parents of students in their classrooms.

The next step is to mention the blog site in various public forums and events.

Mention the Site in Multiple Public Forums

I promoted my blog site by demonstrating it in several public school board meetings so that the local press would pick up on it. The local papers followed by writing articles about the blog. I also mentioned it in various Kiwanis Club and Rotary Club presentations to get the word out among community leaders. You can also advertise it in various school newsletters that go home to parents. For at least a year or more, you will want to continually mention the blog site in as many public forums as possible. I also made a habit of mentioning the blog in as many individual conversations as I could.

In addition to promoting the blog in various settings, you will want to develop your blog site by connecting it to as many other sites as possible. The goal is to make your blog a central site where people can then move on to other sites of interest.

Make Your Site a "One-Stop-Shop"

Good blogs are gateways to rich information from one site. Consider putting on your blog links to all your parent grade portals, school websites, local newspapers, weather channels, athletic links, school calendars, etc. The more links you can provide, the greater chance that a patron will come to your site first. If your site becomes their first stop, they can then move on to other sites of interest. Think about the popularity of the "big box" super stores like Wal-Mart and the small gas station on the corner of the intersection that carries a wide variety of snacks and drinks. What do they have in common? Convenience is what they have in common. In today's fast paced world, consumers appreciate making one stop completing multiple errands at the same time.

If you make your blog a portal to other sources of information such as weather forecasts, athletic events, school announcements, and links to local and national news sources, you may find that your patrons are making your site their first stop whenever they surf the Internet. Remember the power of the blogosphere. If you don't know what sites they wish to click through to, then just ask them. That can be your post for the day. Then take the popular ones and make the selections a mini-poll. See how easy it is?

Once you have increased the number of links to potential sites of interest, you can consider putting an RSS feed on your blog site.

RSS Feeds

The term RSS stands for Really Simple Syndication, although there is really nothing simple about it. Many high end Internet users have so many sites of interest that they do not have time to check each site separately to see if there is anything new or interesting there. So the solution is to choose a news aggregator, which is a news site that will allow you to customize all the sites of particular interest to you. By placing an RSS feed on your blog site, a feature your blog platform will usually provide for you, you will be allowing the reader to place that RSS feed into their news aggregator.

This news aggregator will contact the reader whenever an RSS feed notifies them that a site has updated their information. In this way a busy person can log on each day to their news aggregator site and it will notify them if any of their sites of interest have updated their website.

In addition to the above tips that come from personal experience, the following tips from Darren Rowse (2008) will help the new blogger to further build their readership.

Tips for Finding Readers

1. Write pillar articles and post these articles to your website. A pillar article is an article that is aimed at teaching your readers something. It could be practical tips or suggestions on something that your readers might find interesting. How-to articles seem to have long-term appeal to readers and provide a constant source of information. In an educational setting you might have a series of pillar articles on how to register for school, how to access student grades on the student web portal for grades, or how to sign up to speak at a public school board meeting. These "pillar" articles should contain information that will remain relatively stable and share the type of things that community members might routinely access when they need to know something. A pillar article will bring people to your site over and over when they are searching for specific information about your school district. It could be that your blog site simply links to other information already posted on your school or district's website.

2. Use a logical domain name. When people get ready to access your blog they are not likely to remember the name of the

URL unless it is somehow representative of the name of the blog. When people are talking to their friends about your blog it helps if the domain name is easy to remember.

3. Encourage people to make comments on your blog site. This one is difficult for school administrators because comments can be negative at times. It is important to remember that a little controversy will actually drive traffic to your site. It is simply a part of human nature to be interested in a little controversy or conflict from time to time. Don't be too afraid of it.

4. Write at least one blog post per day. Daily blogging is where it's at. If you don't blog regularly, people have no reason to check in regularly. Your visitors will only stop by a few times before the blog reader decides whether or not to return again. When they stop by and find new information each time they are more likely to return.

I have told you about what works, let me show you in chapter five what doesn't work.

5

HOW TO MAKE YOUR BLOG A DOG

I have reviewed the basics of blogging, the benefits to blogging, and a variety of strategies to consider when creating and marketing your blog. Now we will show you what not to do. The following ideas are sure to make your blog a dog.

WRITE IN SUPERINTENDENT MEMO MODE

All you have to do to make your blog a dog is to write your blog posts in superintendent memo mode. This is guaranteed to virtually kill any lingering interest in your blog site. Most successful blogs are fairly informal in style, even bordering on chatty. The language and style is meant to be engaging and even edgy at times. Most educators have been trained to write formally and administrators with many years of writing formal memorandums could find the informal style of blogging to be difficult. On the other hand, unleashing the inner blogger within could be refreshing. If writing in formal memo mode doesn't kill your blog, then posting infrequently will certainly stop it.

POST INFREQUENTLY

Most good bloggers post every day and the more successful bloggers even post multiple times a day. The purpose for this is to provide new content every time a reader stops by. When a reader sees new content every time they visit, they are reinforced. This is the power of intermittent reinforcement. When a blog reader returns to your site and finds something different or new, it encourages more frequent visits. The day I had seventy-one thousand hits on the website, it was driven partly by controversial comments from visitors and partly by the sheer volume of new comments. There were only twenty-one thousand computers accessing the blog site that day but they were returning over and over again because every time they clicked on the site there was a new comment from a patron. This reinforced their efforts and encouraged them to return looking for new content or new comments from others.

All you have to do to make your blog a dog is to post something once a week or once a month and no one will visit you unless by accident.

If posting in superintendent memo mode or posting infrequently doesn't finish off your blog, then refusing to link to other Internet sources will do it.

DON'T LINK

Most successful blogs use the power of linking to other Internet sources virtually every day. By providing links to other newspapers, blogs, and websites you are using the power and cross-fertilization capabilities of the Internet. Unfortunately, many educators have grown up with the idea that unless they create it or write it themselves, then it isn't valued. The great thing about the blogosphere is that you don't have to be the great creator of all content. You just have to be the source for linking to great content. Linking to other people's sites is encouraged and rewarded. Don't be surprised when you put a hyperlink to another blog on the side bar of your site to see your own blog link show up on their side bar. Bloggers often reward each other by cross-linking to each other's websites.

As a practicing superintendent I often linked to various online newspaper articles and simply added an opinion or a few comments. In most cases my posts were fairly short but linked to other posts with additional content and pictures.

If these tricks don't make your blog a dog then you can always try being boring and hide your sense of humor.

HIDE YOUR SENSE OF HUMOR

Everyone enjoys a good laugh now and then. Showing your lighter side will bring people to your site very quickly. And you don't have to be a comedian to do this. You just have to link to other comedians. In my "Friday's Funnies" posts I often posted funny stories from our own teachers or from my own experiences as a teacher and administrator. However, I often surfed the Internet for funny school stories and either linked to the site with a great story or posted the content on my own site after cutting and pasting the stories into my blog.

Just remember, if you want to make your blog a dog then make sure you hide your funny bone. If hiding the old funny bone doesn't do it then you can always insult your patrons by talking down to them.

TALK DOWN TO THEM

Another sure fire method for killing your blog site is to talk down to your patrons. They may already expect this from you, after all you are a highly trained educational expert and they come to the blog with some preconceived notions and perhaps a few stereotypes about what the educational leader is like. Go ahead and reinforce this by using big words and beating around the bush without saying what you really think. Talk down to them, hide your human side, and make sure you put the patrons in their place. This will make your blog a dog in a hurry.

EYE Z A GR8 BLOGGER

High school students can speak in text lingo but educational leaders trying to be bloggers may be expected to speak in full sentences. Don't be tempted with this one. Don't try to be too hip or to come across in a way that isn't genuine. Just be yourself.

STEAL OTHER BLOGGER'S CONTENT AND POST IT ON YOUR BLOG

I think it is great that you like what someone wrote on their blog so why don't you leave it there. Link to it. Click on the little hyperlink sign on your blog software and cut and paste the URL into your link. Then visitors to your site can click over to the other site. You don't have to be the great originator of all content. Sometimes you just need to learn how to link to other people's content. Besides it's even easier than pretending it was your own. You can make your blog a dog in a hurry if other bloggers see you stealing their content without credit in some way.

If none of the above has killed off your blog then you can always try writing comments and posting content when you're mad. This may do the trick.

WRITE WHEN YOU'RE ANGRY

Every blogger has to develop thick skin over time. But no matter how thick your skin is, there will always be a patron that knows just how to get under it. In many cases you will learn to recognize the style of writing of this patron because they will be a frequent visitor. Sometimes for one reason or another they will do everything they can to push your buttons. Sometimes you may even expect them to be an employee posing as an anonymous visitor. Don't take the bait, unless of course your goal is to make your blog a dog. Writing a post when you are angry is a sure way to offend someone.

Don't interact with them when you are angry unless you have someone else previewing your posts before publishing them. I routinely had a few trusted individuals in my office screen my posts before I submitted them. They usually offered a few suggestions to make the response clearer or less strident.

These tongue-in-cheek suggestions are guaranteed to make your blog a dog. Hopefully you will avoid these disasters and stick to what works.

6

TIPS FOR BLOGGING SUCCESSFULLY

There are a number of common characteristics to most successful blog sites. When you decide to start blogging, Darren Rowse (2008) from ProBlogger.com suggests you ask yourself the following questions before you hit the "publish" button.

NINE ESSENTIAL QUESTIONS TO ASK YOURSELF BEFORE POSTING TO YOUR BLOG

1. Does this post give something unique and useful to my readers?
2. Will it enhance their lives in some way or is it just fluff?
3. Is the spelling correct?
4. Does the post make sense grammatically?
5. How could I make the post easier to scan for readers? (headings, formatting, images, etc.)
6. Is the title engaging? Does it draw people to the post?

7. Could I give this post a little more time before publishing to mature? Would coming back to it tomorrow help me to add depth to it?
8. Have I written on this topic before and can I link to it?

HOW TO BUILD COMMUNITY ON YOUR BLOG

Rowse (2008) also offers these tips on his blog site for building a sense of community with your blog readers and I expanded some of them to make them more relevant to the school setting.

1. Ask questions. The key to more comments and interaction on your blog is to ask your community more questions. Just remember, if you seek their input you need to respect their attempts to give it, even if it isn't what you want to hear.
2. Give your readers homework. Interestingly enough, giving your readers homework to do is often a very interactive process. You might be surprised how much time readers will spend researching and reading about various questions you pose.
3. Respond to reader's questions and comments. There is nothing more reinforcing than when the chief blogger answers a specific patron's question on the blog site. There may not be a more powerful use of the blog than this one. As a blogging school administrator I would often respond to a patron's question with a separate post. My rationale was that if one patron had that question then undoubtedly others did too.
4. Make readers famous. Whenever possible point out and celebrate your readers publicly.

In addition to these tips for blogging successfully, good bloggers have developed the knack for using attractive titles for their blog posts.

USING BLOG POST TITLES SUCCESSFULLY

There are many ways that bloggers can call attention to their posts but most of these are related to the way the posts are titled. Because of the way search engines work, it is important to have a good title for your blog post.

1. Make the title catchy. Good titles draw people's attention. Your catchy title may shock people or it may allude to a controversy or it may simply leave them wondering. In any case it should leave them with an interest in reading a little further to see what you have to say.
2. Use key words. Most search engines will use the main words in your title. If people are surfing the web looking for information on a topic it helps if your title has included the key words that a person is likely to enter into the search engine. This is a common way of finding new readers outside of your area.
3. Keep the title simple. While catchy titles are often effective, it is often the simple, short, and self-explanatory title that is easy for the patron to locate through a search engine.

OTHER TIPS

Griff Wigley of Wigley and Associates (n.d.) offers a number of ideas on his blog site for helping the leader with their own blogging. Many of Griff's ideas were remixed and are included in the ideas listed below. For more information on Griff's blogging tutorial you can follow this link (wigleyandassociates.com/leadership-blogging-guide) to the blog tutorial on his website.

1. Use a series of posts: As an educational leader you may have a lot to say but don't try to say it all at once. Consider

running a series on specific topics such as school discipline, food service, transportation, school funding, property taxes, construction projects, curriculum revision, new testing requirements, etc. Most search engines really like posts that have one topic with numerous key words in it. Don't try to educate the public on multiple issues in one post. Bloggers refer to this as "granular" posting. In other words, the entire post is specific to one topic. You can, however, run a series of posts that address various aspects of a complex issue.

2. Use pictures when possible: Pictures are easy to post and often tell a great story that words cannot express. Just remember not to violate your own Internet use policy when you post them. I once posted a picture of a student that was not an athlete and a commenter was quick to point out that I was violating our own board-adopted Internet usage policy. I had to admit my wrongdoing and pull the picture. I then had to go on to explain the legal reasons why pictures of athletes in action were not a violation of the Internet usage policy or an invasion of privacy, an issue that has already been litigated numerous times. Pictures often speak far more eloquently then our words do.

3. Write with a personal touch: This is perhaps the most important aspect of blogging, especially for the educational leader. If your personality doesn't shine through your writing, then your blog will not be any more interesting than your school newsletter. Not that your particular school newsletter is boring of course, just that blogs tend to be more personal.

4. Answer reader e-mail questions by posting your responses on the blog: It is safe to assume that if one reader has a question about something, then others probably do too. By answering their questions in a blog post, you not only help

inform others but you give a sense of legitimacy to the person with the question. Of course, if the e-mailed question is of a personal nature or not appropriate for a public response then you would answer them privately instead. I have always found that patrons appreciated the post. Especially if I did so in a confidential manner that did not call attention to them personally.

5. Tell your readers when you will not be posting: Every blogger needs a break now and then. You can either post your intentions by letting them know that you will not be posting for the next week, or you could choose to name a guest blogger and have the site stay active. By posting your intentions to be gone, you will build trust with your readers. If they were to stop by your site three days in a row and find nothing new, they might choose not to return. But if they know you will not be blogging for a week or so then it will not be a problem.

6. Tell stories: Wrigley (2005) says that storytelling in written form can be a very compelling way of getting a message out and even has some advantages over oral storytelling.

   • Your audience-of-many is always available.
   • A blog post (via its PermaLink) can get easily passed around via the web and e-mail.
   • The PermaLink of the blog post never dies. If your story turns out to have long-lasting impact, its web address can be linked to indefinitely.

   Weblog storytelling tips:

   • The real names of people involved can help to make the story. Include them, with their permission. Frame your story with time/date, such as "yesterday . . ." "earlier this morning . . ." "last Tuesday . . ."
   • Describe the place, or at least name it. If you don't have the time or skill to "set the scene," it can help to use a

photo. There's hardly a blog post that can't include some elements of storytelling. Imagine yourself talking to a colleague or friend about what it is you're blogging and then bring that tone to your post.

7. Give us a reason to come back to your blog site: Why don't you tease us with an upcoming feature or topic? Tell us about where you are headed next. Give us a reason why we should stop by your site for another visit. Too many blogs simply ramble on about whatever is on the blogger's mind but give us no specific reason why we should return.

8. Write and spell correctly: If you are an educational leader, nothing will get you in trouble faster than making a spelling mistake. I once made the mistake of sending an e-mail to a patron without clicking on spell check. What a big mistake that was. The return e-mail went clear off-topic and focused on my spelling and/or typing problems as an educational leader. I don't think I ever sent out an e-mail or published a blog topic again without at least running spell check. Educators will not catch a break in this area from the public. You are the leader of educators. Check your spelling and grammar on every single post you make.

9. Teach me: Opinions are great, but most of your public likes learning things. Remember that you are a prominent educational leader in your community, so unless you are a gifted commentator, satirist, and editorialist with the gift of gab and opinion, then teach us, but do it kindly and without arrogance.

10. Make your visitors think: The biggest problem with most blogs is the lack of interaction with the audience. If your blog is nothing more than an electronic newsletter, then just stick it on your website and be done with it. If you aren't going to provoke your audience to think about some-

thing and interact with your ideas, then post on the school website and forget about it.

Another blog expert is Dr. Scott McLeod, who has spearheaded several blogging initiatives aimed at helping school administrators understand the benefits to blogging. This is a blog topic he posted on his blog, "Dangerously Irrelevant" (www.dangerously irrelevant.org/2007/01/how_do_i_blog_t.html).

Like everyone else, I blog on stuff that crosses my radar screen. My ideas might come from electronic sources such as blogs, web sites, podcasts, etc. or they might come from more traditional print resources. I probably tap into some literature sources that most other edubloggers don't. For example, I not only live in the educational blogosphere but I also live in the world of educational leadership academia, research, and practice. Accordingly, I'm reading educational administrator practitioner magazines and research journals, attending conferences, listening to academic presentations, staying in touch with all of the major educational leadership and educational research associations, and so on. Good print and/or local resources can be excellent idea generators for blog posts and go beyond the same education blogs that we all read.

Sometimes I'll see something that someone else did and feel that I can add some value to it rather than just post about it. My recent modifications of Karl Fisch's Did You Know? video and Christian Long's Future of Learning manifesto are examples of this. So is the aggregation of various quotes from the blogosphere that I did last September. When I'm 'adding value' to something it's because I need it in a different format for my own teaching or presentation purposes, not because the original is inferior.

Finally, I try to be somewhat intentional and proactive about what I blog rather than just being reactive. For example, my two series last fall on blogging for administrators and gaming, cognition, and education were both planned well in advance of the actual blog posts occurring. I like to identify areas of need for administrators and other educators and then try to create resources that I think will help them. I am a strong believer that we need to be creating resources for educators to help them in their jobs, not just pontificating.

So there it is: nothing earth-shattering. I think the key is to write passionately about stuff that interests you. If it fires you up, it will fire others up too and they will find you and stay with you. Remember that you don't always need to come up with 'original content.' Adding a new perspective to others' content or making interesting connections across others' content also works quite well. Don't forget to use all of the tools at your disposal to publicize your blog: Technorati tags, Feedburner tools, frequent comments on others' posts, creative post titles, trackbacks, blogrolls, begging, etc. It all helps.

WHY BLOG?

Blogging is just one more tool for the communication-oriented school leader. It will not replace conventional public relations strategies, nor is it a good choice when the leader is already under siege. Yet it remains a very powerful tool for interacting with the community in a high tech age. Our constituents are growing accustomed to communicating in a fast-paced digital world. The more avenues you can provide to educate and inform the public about the important issues that affect our schools and our children, the better chance we have of sustaining and improving our public schools. Remember this, "If you don't start blogging to them, they may just start blogging about you!"

7

THE VISION

IMAGINE THIS

Picture in your mind a very large, colorful, three-dimensional map of the United States of America with a colored push pin placed on the map at the precise location of the home office of each public school superintendent and school administrator in America. Now let's assume for a moment that each of these administrators had bought into the notion that blogging at some level was a useful tool in their overall communication plan.

Imagine that each of these administrators had developed a small but loyal group of daily and weekly visitors to their own unique blog site. Assume that each blog site had hundreds or even thousands of weekly blog visitors. Now try to picture a series of lines going out from the push pin location of the administrator's home office to the home location of each visitor. Assume for a moment that many of these blogging school leaders had cross-linked to other interesting bloggers and therefore visitors of some blogs were now becoming regular visitors to other blogs.

In my mind this vision quickly becomes an intricate maze all across America. The power of this vision comes from the social networking potential provided by the Internet. This phenomenon has begun to influence everything from politics to consumer spending.

Why is this vision compelling and powerful? I have tried throughout this book to build the case that blogging and other forms of social networking are changing the nature of interactions across the world. Information, news, rumors, and gossip can fly across these networks at the speed of light.

How can the savvy school leader harness and utilize this technology in a preventative fashion? Or, will school administrators sit back passively and find themselves steamrolled by local bloggers themselves? Well, not if Dr. Scott McLeod can help it. He is one blogger, professor, and visionary who "gets it." Dr. McLeod was helpful in launching the Principal Blogging Project, designed to expand the number of school administrators who blog.

PRINCIPAL BLOGGING PROJECT

The Principal Blogging Project, as described on their website, (www.schooltechleadership.org/principalbloggingproject/) is a new initiative to help principals tap into the power of blogging. They will create a free blog for any principal interested in using these new communication tools. If you are a principal interested in blogging, participating in this project is easy!

Step 1—Download and read the information packet (includes: Why Blog as an Administrator?).

Step 2—Complete the online sign-up form.

Step 3—Wait to receive an e-mail from us with further information about your blog, instructions on how to post, etc.

The Principal Blogging Project is an initiative of the UCEA Center for the Advanced Study of Technology Leadership in Education (CASTLE), the nation's only university center dedicated to the technology needs of school administrators. The Principal Project provides resources for principals who blog, along with simplified instructions for getting started. They even provide a running list of other principal blogs so you can get ideas for your own blog.

If building principals and central office administrators were to embrace the vision of interacting with the greater public in a massive blogging network across America, perhaps the greatest potential impact would be in the political arena of educational policymaking.

POLITICAL INFLUENCE

The involvement of the federal government through the legislation called No Child Left Behind (NCLB) was the largest and most invasive attempt to impact public education in each state since special education laws were passed. While the benefits to NCLB remain hotly debated today, there is general agreement among school leaders that there was not a lot of grassroots involvement among the public on this legislation.

Imagine if the large blogging network described above was a reality today. Do you think this network could be useful in influencing state and federal legislation affecting public education? Just think if every school leader blogged about the pros and cons to how such legislation could affect the local school district and local parents. Just imagine how much grassroots activism and involvement in the legislative process would increase if an informed public could simply click on your blog site link and e-mail their personal legislator regarding their opinions on a particular bill.

At the current time it is widely recognized that professional lobbyists are the primary influencers on policymaking at the state and national level. Yet, most legislators will respond to massive input from voters who actually determine their fate.

The problem is that grassroots political activism takes time and effort. The voter first of all needs to know who their legislators are and how they can reach them.

In my vision of an overarching social network of blogging leaders across America, I can see a day when most of America could drop an e-mail to a legislator with no more than a few mouse clicks from the superintendent's blog site. After all, across large swaths of America, the local school leader is the most prominent figure in the public eye. If not us, then who will do it?

No other group of leaders in America has such a massive responsibility to virtually every child, parent, and taxpayer in America as do school administrators. It is time to harness the power of the new technology and build our networks to the American public through interacting, informing, educating, listening, and engaging the American public through blogging.

IT'S TIME TO ACT—NOT JUST REACT

Let's face it. Most administrators find themselves reacting to the crisis of the day and seldom carve out enough time to plan for the future. But the onslaught on public education has reached the point where the very essence of what public education has stood for is under attack. Public education has always been the great equalizer in a democratic society but currently the very fabric of public education has worn thin to the point where its mandate lies in jeopardy. It is time for school administrators to build their networks and involve the public in the political process.

For the skeptics out there I would say this. You can't roll this technology backwards. It is here to stay in some form or another. Blogging as we know it may take on new forms as technology continues to advance, but the fact remains, some form of social networking appears to be here to stay.

Administrators can either embrace it for good and use the forum in a preventative way to get our messages out, or we can sit back and be buried by those who would use the technology against public education.

Blogging may not be the answer to all the communication problems in public education, but in the hands of a capable school administrator, it certainly can be a useful tool in the overall communication plan for your school or school district.

Good luck and get started!

It may be a blog-eat-blog world but now you know what you need in order to thrive as a school administrator in today's high tech world.

REFERENCES

Principal Blogging Project. (n.d.) Retrieved May 26, 2008 from www.schooltechleadership.org/principalbloggingproject.

Quoteland.com. (2006.) Retrieved May 28, 2008 from forum.quoteland .com/1/OpenTopic?a=tpc&s=586192041&f=099191541&m=4031943806.

Rowse, D. (2008). Retrieved May 28, 2008 from www.problogger.net/ archives/2008/04/26/how-to-build-community-on-your-blog.

Rowse, D. (2008). Retrieved May 28, 2008 from www.problogger.net/ archives/2008/04/28/9-essential-questions-to-ask-yourself-before-posting-to-your-blog.

The Wawascene. (n.d.). wawasee.blogspot.com.

Wigley, G. (2005). Guide to Civic Leadership Blogging. Retrieved May 26, 2008 from wigleyandassociates.com/leadership-blogging-guide/ how_to_blog/tell_stories.

Wigley, G. (n.d.). Retrieved May 26, 2008 from wigleyandassociates.com.

ABOUT THE AUTHOR

Dr. Mark J. Stock is currently assistant professor of educational leadership at the University of Wyoming. He has nineteen years of experience as a school administrator, including eleven years as superintendent of schools. He ran a successful and popular blog site called "The Wawascene" for several years as superintendent of schools and lived to tell about it. He is also a contributor to Dr. Scott McLeod's blog, "Leader Talk."

He says, "It's a blog-eat-blog world but the tech savvy superintendent can thrive not just survive in today's communication frenzied world."